Contents

PREFACE

If you've already followed a BTEC First programme, you will know that this is an exciting way to study; if you are fresh from GCSEs you will find that from now on you will be in charge of your own learning. This guide has been written specially for you, to help get you started and then succeed on your BTEC National course.

The **Introduction** concentrates on making sure you have all the right facts about your course at your fingertips. Also, it guides you through the important skills you need to develop if you want to do well including:

- managing your time
- researching information
- preparing a presentation.

Keep this by your side throughout your course and dip into it whenever you need to.

The **Activities** give you tasks to do on your own, in a small group or as a class. They will help you internalise your learning and then prepare for assessment by practising your skills and showing you how much you know. These activities are not for assessment.

The sample **Marked Assignments** show you what other students have done to gain Pass, Merit or Distinction. By seeing what past students have done, you should be able to improve your own grade.

Your BTEC National will cover six, twelve or eighteen units depending on whether you are doing an Award, Certificate or Diploma. In this guide the activities cover sections from Unit 1 – Government, Policies and the Public Services, Unit 2 – Team Leadership in the Uniformed Public Services, Unit 5 – Understanding Discipline within the Uniformed Public Services and Unit 7 – Physical Preparation and Fitness for the Uniformed Services. These units underpin your study of Public Services.

Because the guide covers only four units, it is essential that you do all the other work your tutors set you. You will have to research information in textbooks, in the library and on the Internet. You should have the opportunity to visit local organisations and welcome visiting speakers to your institution. This is a great way to find out more about your chosen vocational area – the type of jobs that are available and what the work is really like.

This Guide is a taster, an introduction to your BTEC National. Use it as such and make the most of the rich learning environment that your tutors will provide for you. Your BTEC National will give you an excellent base for further study, a broad understanding of the public services and the knowledge you need to succeed in the world of work. Remember, thousands of students have achieved a BTEC National and are now studying for a degree or at work, building a successful career.

edexcel
advancing learning, changing lives

BTEC National
Uniformed Public Services

Study Guide

A PEARSON COMPANY

BTEC National Study Guide: Uniformed Public Services

Published by:
Edexcel Limited
One90 High Holborn
London WC1V 7BH
www.edexcel.org.uk

Distributed by:
Pearson Education Limited
Edinburgh Gate
Harlow
Essex CM20 2JE

First published 2007
Second impression 2008
Third impression 2008
Fourth impression 2009

ISBN: 978-1-84690-222-2

Project managed and typeset by Hart McLeod, Cambridge
Printed in Great Britain by Henry Ling Limited, at the Dorset Press, Dorchester, DT1 1HD

Cover image ©Rex Argent/Alamy

The publisher's policy is to use paper manufactured from sustainable forests.

All reasonable efforts have been made to trace and contact original copyright owners.

This material offers high quality support for the delivery of Edexcel qualifications.
This does not mean that it is essential to achieve any Edexcel qualification, nor does it mean that this is the only suitable material available to support any Edexcel qualification. No Edexcel-published material will be used verbatim in setting any Edexcel assessment and any resource lists produced by Edexcel shall include this and other appropriate texts.

Acknowledgements

p.46 ©Michael Betts/Photographer's Choice/Getty Images; p.48 ©PBWPIX/Alamy; p.52 ©Lothar Schulz/fStop/Getty Images; p.89 ©Peter Titmuss/Alamy; p.105 ©Guy Ryecart/Dorling Kindersley/Getty Images; p.116 ©Last Resort/ Photodisc/Getty Images

INTRODUCTION

SEVEN STEPS TO SUCCESS ON YOUR BTEC NATIONAL

You have received this guide because you have decided to do a BTEC National qualification. You may even have started your course. At this stage you should feel good about your decision. BTEC Nationals have many benefits – they are well-known and respected qualifications, they provide excellent preparation for future work or help you to get into university if that is your aim. If you are already at work then gaining a BTEC National will increase your value to your employer and help to prepare you for promotion.

Despite all these benefits though, you may be rather apprehensive about your ability to cope. Or you may be wildly enthusiastic about the whole course! More probably, you are somewhere between the two – perhaps quietly confident most of the time but sometimes worried that you may get out of your depth as the course progresses. You may be certain you made the right choice or still have days when your decision worries you. You may understand exactly what the course entails and what you have to do – or still feel rather bewildered, given all the new stuff you have to get your head around.

Your tutors will use the induction sessions at the start of your course to explain the important information they want you to know. At the time, though, it can be difficult to remember everything. This is especially true if you have just left school and are now studying in a new environment, among a group of people you have only just met. It is often only later that you think of useful questions to ask. Sometimes, misunderstandings or difficulties may only surface weeks or months into a course – and may continue for some time unless they are quickly resolved.

This student guide has been written to help to minimise these difficulties, so that you get the most out of your BTEC National course from day one. You can read through it at your own pace. You can look back at it whenever you have a problem or query.

This Introduction concentrates on making sure you have all the right facts about your course at your fingertips. This includes a **Glossary** (on page 32) which explains the specialist terms you may hear or read – including words and phrases highlighted in bold type in this Introduction.

The Introduction also guides you through the important skills you need to develop if you want to do well – such as managing your time, researching information and preparing a presentation; as well as reminding you about the key skills you will need to do justice to your work, such as good written and verbal communications.

Make sure you have all the right facts

- Use the PlusPoint boxes in each section to help you to stay focused on the essentials.

- Use the Action Point boxes to check out things you need to know or do right now.

- Refer to the Glossary (on page 32) if you need to check the meaning of any of the specialist terms you may hear or read.

Remember, thousands of students have achieved BTEC National Diplomas and are now studying for a degree or at work, building a successful career. Many were nervous and unsure of themselves at the outset – and very few experienced absolutely no setbacks during the course. What they did have, though, was a belief in their own ability to do well if they concentrated on getting things right one step at a time. This Introduction enables you to do exactly the same!

STEP ONE

UNDERSTAND YOUR COURSE AND HOW IT WORKS

What is a BTEC qualification and what does it involve? What will you be expected to do on the course? What can you do afterwards? How does this National differ from 'A' levels or a BTEC First qualification?

All these are common questions – but not all prospective students ask them! Did you? And, if so, did you really listen to the answers? And can you remember them now?

If you have already completed a BTEC First course then you may know some of the answers – although you may not appreciate some of the differences between that course and your new one.

Let's start by checking out the basics.

- All BTEC National qualifications are **vocational** or **work-related**. This doesn't mean that they give you all the skills that you need to do a job. It does mean that you gain the specific knowledge and understanding relevant to your chosen subject or area of work. This means that when you start in a job you will learn how to do the work more quickly and should progress further. If you are already employed, it means you become more valuable to your employer. You can choose to study a BTEC National in a wide range of vocational areas, such as Business, Health and Social Care, IT, Performing Arts and many others.

- There are three types of BTEC National qualification and each has a different number of units.

  - The BTEC National Award usually has 6 units and takes 360 **guided learning hours (GLH)** to complete. It is often offered as a part-time or short course but you may be one of the many students doing an Award alongside A-levels as a full-time course. An Award is equivalent to one 'A' level.

  - The BTEC National Certificate usually has 12 units and takes 720 GLH to complete. You may be able to study for the Certificate on a part-time or full-time course. It is equivalent to two 'A' levels.

– The BTEC National Diploma usually has 18 units and takes 1080 GLH to complete. It is normally offered as a two-year full-time course. It is equivalent to three 'A' levels.

These qualifications are often described as **nested**. This means that they fit inside each other (rather like Russian dolls!) because the same units are common to them all. This means that if you want to progress from one to another you can do so easily by simply completing more units.

- Every BTEC National qualification has a set number of **core units**. These are the compulsory units every student must complete. The number of core units you will do on your course depends upon the vocational area you are studying.

- All BTEC National qualifications also have a range of **specialist units** from which you may be able to make a choice. These enable you to study particular areas in more depth.

- Some BTEC National qualifications have **specialist core units**. These are mandatory units you will have to complete if you want to follow a particular pathway in certain vocational areas. Engineering is an example of a qualification with the over-arching title, Engineering, which has a set of core units that all students must complete. Then, depending what type of engineering a student wants to follow, there are more specialist core units that must be studied.

- On all BTEC courses you are expected to be in charge of your own learning. If you have completed a BTEC First, you will already have been introduced to this idea, but you can expect the situation to be rather different now that you are working at BTEC National level. Students on a BTEC First course will be expected to need more guidance whilst they develop their skills and find their feet. In some cases, this might last quite some time. On a BTEC National course you will be expected to take more responsibility for yourself and your own learning almost from the outset. You will quickly be expected to start thinking for yourself. This means planning what to do and carrying out a task without needing constant reminders. This doesn't mean that your tutor won't give you help and guidance when you need it. It does mean, though, that you need to be 'self-starting' and to be able to use your own initiative. You also need to be able to assess your own performance and make improvements when necessary. If you enjoy having the freedom to make your own decisions and work at your own pace then you will welcome this type of learning with open arms. However, there are dangers! If you are a procrastinator (look up this word if you don't know what it means!) then it's quite likely you will quickly get in a muddle. In this case read Step 3 – Use your time wisely – very carefully indeed!

- The way you are assessed and graded on a BTEC course is different from an 'A' level course, although you will still obtain UCAS points which you need if you want to go to university. You can read about this in the next section.

PLUSPOINTS	ACTION POINTS

PLUSPOINTS

+ You can usually choose to study part-time or full-time for your BTEC National and do an Award, Certificate or Diploma and progress easily from one to the other.

+ You will study both core units and specialist units on your course.

+ When you have completed your BTEC course you can get a job (or **apprenticeship**), use your qualification to develop your career and/or continue your studies to degree level.

+ You are responsible for your own learning on a BTEC course. This prepares you for life at work or at university when you will be expected to be self-starting and to use your own initiative.

ACTION POINTS

✓ Check you know whether you are studying for an Award, Certificate or Diploma and find out the number of units you will be studying for your BTEC National qualification.

✓ Find out which are core and which are specialist units, and which specialist units are offered at your school or college.

✓ Check out the length of your course and when you will be studying each unit.

✓ Explore the Edexcel website at www.edexcel.org.uk. Your first task is to find what's available for your particular BTEC National qualification. Start by finding National qualifications, then look for your vocational area and check you are looking at the 2007 schemes. Then find the specification for your course. Don't print this out – it is far too long. You could, of course, save it if you want to refer to it regularly or you could just look through it for interest and then bookmark the pages relating to your qualification for future reference.

✓ Score yourself out of 5 (where 0 is awful and 5 is excellent) on each of the following to see how much improvement is needed for you to become responsible for your own learning!

Being punctual; organisational ability; tidiness; working accurately; finding and correcting own mistakes; solving problems; accepting responsibility; working with details; planning how to do a job; using own initiative; thinking up new ideas; meeting deadlines.

✓ Draw up your own action plan to improve any areas where you are weak. Talk this through at your next individual **tutorial**.

STEP TWO

UNDERSTAND HOW YOU ARE ASSESSED AND GRADED – AND USE THIS KNOWLEDGE TO YOUR ADVANTAGE!

If you already have a BTEC First qualification, you may think that you don't need to read this section because you assume that BTEC National is simply more of the same. Whilst there are some broad similarities, you will now be working at an entirely different level and the grades you get for your work could be absolutely crucial to your future plans.

Equally, if you have opted for BTEC National rather than 'A' level because you thought you would have less work (or writing) to do then you need to read this section very carefully. Indeed, if you chose your BTEC National because you thought it would guarantee you an easy life, you are likely to get quite a shock when reality hits home!

It is true that, unlike 'A' levels, there are no exams on a BTEC course. However, to do well you need to understand the importance of your assignments, how these are graded and how these convert into unit points and UCAS points. This is the focus of this section.

Your assignments

On a BTEC National course your learning is assessed by means of **assignments** set by your tutors and given to you to complete throughout your course.

■ Your tutors will use a variety of **assessment methods**, such as case studies, projects, presentations and shows to obtain evidence of your skills and knowledge to date. You may also be given work-based or **time-constrained** assignments – where your performance might be observed and assessed. It will depend very much on the vocational area you are studying (see also page 16).

■ Important skills you will need to learn are how to research information (see page 25) and how to use your time effectively, particularly if you have to cope with several assignments at the same time (see page 12). You may also be expected to work cooperatively as a member of a team to complete some parts of your assignments – especially if you are doing a subject like Performing Arts – or to prepare a presentation (see page 26).

■ All your assignments are based on **learning outcomes** set by Edexcel. These are listed for each unit in your course specification. You have to meet *all* the learning outcomes to pass the unit.

Your grades

On a BTEC National course, assignments that meet the learning outcomes are graded as Pass, Merit or Distinction.

■ The difference between these grades has very little to do with how much you write! Edexcel sets out the **grading criteria** for the different grades in a **grading grid**. This identifies the **higher-level skills** you have to demonstrate to earn a higher grade. You can find out more about this, and read examples of good (and not so good) answers to assignments at Pass, Merit and Distinction level in the marked assignments section starting on page 121. You will also find out more about getting the best grade you can in Step 5 – Understand your assessment – on page 16.

■ Your grades for all your assignments earn you **unit points**. The number of points you get for each unit is added together and your total score determines your final grade(s) for the qualification – again either Pass, Merit or Distinction. You get one final grade if you are taking a BTEC National Award, two if you are taking a BTEC National Certificate and three if you are taking a BTEC National Diploma.

■ Your points and overall grade(s) also convert to **UCAS points** which you will need if you want to apply to study on a degree course. As an example, if you are studying a BTEC National Diploma, and achieve three final pass grades you will achieve 120 UCAS points. If you achieve three final distinction grades the number of UCAS points you have earned goes up to 360.

■ It is important to note that you start earning both unit and UCAS points from the very first assignment you complete! This means that if you take a long time to settle into your course, or to start working productively, you could easily lose valuable points for quite some time. If you have your heart set on a particular university or degree course then this could limit your choices. Whichever way you look at it, it is silly to squander potentially good grades for an assignment and their equivalent points, just because you didn't really understand what you had to do – which is why this guide has been written to help you!

■ If you take a little time to understand how **grade boundaries** work, you can see where you need to concentrate your efforts to get the best final grade possible. Let's give a simple example. Chris and Shaheeda both want to go to university and have worked hard on their BTEC National Diploma course. Chris ends with a total score of 226 unit points which converts to 280 UCAS points. Shaheeda ends with a total score of 228 unit points – just two points more – which converts to 320 UCAS points! This is because a score of between 204 and 227 unit points gives 280 UCAS points, whereas a score of 228 – 251 points gives 320 UCAS points. Shaheeda is pleased because this increases her chances of getting a place on the degree course she wants. Chris is annoyed. He says if he had known then he would have put more effort into his last assignment to get two points more.

- It is always tempting to spend time on work you like doing, rather than work you don't – but this can be a mistake if you have already done the best you can at an assignment and it would already earn a very good grade. Instead you should now concentrate on improving an assignment which covers an area where you know you are weak, because this will boost your overall grade(s). You will learn more about this in Step 3 – Use your time wisely.

PLUSPOINTS

+ Your learning is assessed in a variety of ways, such as by assignments, projects and case studies. You will need to be able to research effectively, manage your own time and work well with other people to succeed.

+ You need to demonstrate specific knowledge and skills to achieve the learning outcomes set by Edexcel. You need to demonstrate you can meet all the learning outcomes to pass a unit.

+ Higher-level skills are required for higher grades. The grading criteria for Pass, Merit and Distinction grades are set out in a grading grid for the unit.

+ The assessment grades of Pass, Merit and Distinction convert to unit points. The total number of unit points you receive during the course determines your final overall grade(s) and the UCAS points you have earned.

+ Working effectively from the beginning maximises your chances of achieving a good qualification grade. Understanding grade boundaries enables you to get the best final grade(s) possible.

ACTION POINTS

✓ Find the learning outcomes for the units you are currently studying. Your tutor may have given you these already, or you can find them in the specification for your course that you already accessed at www.edexcel.org.uk.

✓ Look at the grading grid for the units and identify the way the evidence required changes to achieve the higher grades. Don't worry if there are some words that you do not understand – these are explained in more detail on page 32 of this guide.

✓ If you are still unsure how the unit points system works, ask your tutor to explain it to you.

✓ Check out the number of UCAS points you would need for any course or university in which you are interested.

✓ Keep a record of the unit points you earn throughout your course and check regularly how this is affecting your overall grade(s), based on the grade boundaries for your qualification. Your tutor will give you this information or you can check it yourself in the specification for your course on the Edexcel website.

STEP THREE

USE YOUR TIME WISELY

Most students on a BTEC National course are trying to combine their course commitments with a number of others – such as a job (either full or part-time) and family responsibilities. In addition, they still want time to meet with friends, enjoy a social life and keep up hobbies and interests that they have.

Starting the course doesn't mean that you have to hide away for months if you want to do well. It does mean that you have to use your time wisely if you want to do well, stay sane and keep a balance in your life.

You will only do this if you make time work for you, rather than against you, by taking control. This means that you decide what you are doing, when you are doing it and work purposefully; rather than simply reacting to problems or panicking madly because you've yet another deadline staring you in the face.

Use your time wisely

This becomes even more important as your course progresses because your workload is likely to increase, particularly towards the end of a term. In the early days you may be beautifully organised and able to cope easily. Then you may find you have several tasks to complete simultaneously as well as some research to start. Then you get two assignments in the same week from different tutors – as well as having a presentation to prepare. Then another assignment is scheduled for the following week – and so on. This is not because your tutors are being deliberately difficult. Indeed, most will try to schedule your assignments to avoid such clashes. The problem, of course, is that none of your tutors can assess your abilities until you have learned something – so if several units start and end at the same time it is highly likely there will be some overlap between your assignments.

To cope when the going gets tough, without collapsing into an exhausted heap, you need to learn a few time management skills.

- **Pinpoint where your time goes at the moment** Time is like money – it's usually difficult to work out where it all went! Work out how much time you currently spend at college, at work, at home and on social activities. Check, too, how much time you waste each week – and why this happens. Are you disorganised or do you easily get distracted? Then identify commitments that are vital and those that are optional so that you know where you can find time if you need to.

- **Plan when and where to work** It is unrealistic not to expect to do quite a lot of work for your course in your own time. It is also better to work regularly, and in relatively short bursts, than to work just once or twice a week for very long stretches. In addition to deciding when to work, and for how long, you also need to think about when and where to work. If you are a lark, you will work better early in the day; if you are an owl, you will be at your best later on. Whatever time you work, you need somewhere quiet so that you can concentrate and with space for books and other resources you need. If the words 'quiet oasis' and 'your house' are totally incompatible at any time of the day or night then check out the opening hours of your local and college library so that you have an escape route if you need it. If you are trying to combine studying with parental responsibilities it is sensible to factor in your children's commitments – and work around their bedtimes too! Store up favours, too, from friends and grandparents that you can call in if you get desperate for extra time when an assignment deadline is looming.

- **Schedule your commitments** Keep a diary or (even better) a wall chart and write down every appointment you make or task you are given. It is useful to use a colour code to differentiate between personal and work or course commitments. You may also want to enter assignment review dates with your tutor in one colour and final deadline dates in another. Keep your diary or chart up-to-date by adding any new dates promptly every time you receive another task or assignment or whenever you make any other arrangements. Keep checking ahead so that you always have prior warning when important dates are looming. This stops you from planning a heavy social week when you will be at your busiest at work or college and from arranging a dental appointment on the morning when you and your team are scheduled to give an important presentation!

- **Prioritise your work** This means doing the most important and urgent task first, rather than the one you like the most! Normally this will be the task or assignment with the nearest deadline. There are two exceptions. Sometimes you may need to send off for information and allow time for it to arrive. It is therefore sensible to do this first so that you are not held up later. The second is when you have to take account of other people's schedules – because you are working in a team or are arranging to interview someone, for example. In this case you will have to arrange your schedule around their needs, not just your own.

- **Set sensible timescales** Trying to do work at the last minute or in a rush is never satisfactory, so it is wise always to allocate more time than you think you will need, never less. Remember, too, to include all the stages of a complex task or assignment, such as researching the information, deciding what to use, creating a first draft, checking it and making improvements and printing it out. If you are planning to do any of your work in a central facility always allow extra time and try to start work early. If you arrive at the last minute you may find every computer and printer is fully utilised until closing time.

- **Learn self-discipline!** This means not putting things off (procrastinating!) because you don't know where to start or don't feel in the mood. Unless you are ill, you have to find some way of persuading yourself to work. One way is to bribe yourself. Make a start and promise yourself that if you work productively for 30 minutes then you deserve a small reward. After 30 minutes you may have become more engrossed and want to keep going a little longer. Otherwise at least you have made a start, so it's easier to come back and do more later. It doesn't matter whether you have research to do, an assignment to write up, a coaching session to plan, or lines to learn, you need to be self-disciplined.

- **Take regular breaks and keep your life in balance** Don't go to the opposite extreme and work for hours on end. Take regular breaks to give yourself a rest and a change of activity. You need to recharge your batteries! Similarly, don't cancel every social arrangement so that you can work 24/7. Whilst this may be occasionally necessary if you have several deadlines looming simultaneously, it should only be a last resort. If you find yourself doing this regularly then go back to the beginning of this section and see where your time-management planning is going wrong.

PLUSPOINTS

+ Being in control of your time enables you to balance your commitments according to their importance and allows you not let to anyone down – including yourself.

+ Controlling time involves knowing how you spend (and waste!) your time now, planning when best to do work, scheduling your commitments and setting sensible timescales for work to be done.

+ Knowing how to prioritise means that you will schedule work effectively according to its urgency and importance but this also requires self-discipline. You have to follow the schedule you have set for yourself!

+ Managing time and focusing on the task at hand means you will do better work and be less stressed, because you are not having to react to problems or crises. You can also find the time to include regular breaks and leisure activities in your schedule.

ACTION POINTS

✓ Find out how many assignments you can expect to receive this term and when you can expect to receive these. Enter this information into your student diary or onto a planner you can refer to regularly.

✓ Update your diary and/or planner with other commitments that you have this term – both work/college-related and social. Identify any potential clashes and decide the best action to take to solve the problem.

✓ Identify your own best time and place to work quietly and effectively.

✓ Displacement activities are things we do to put off starting a job we don't want to do – such as sending texts, watching TV, checking emails etc. Identify yours so that you know when you're doing them!

STEP FOUR

UTILISE ALL YOUR RESOURCES

Your resources are all the things that can help you to achieve your qualification. They can therefore be as wide-ranging as your favourite website and your **study buddy** (see page 15) who collects handouts for you if you miss a class.

Your college will provide the essential resources for your course, such as a library with a wide range of books and electronic reference sources, learning resource centre(s), the computer network and Internet access. Other basic resources you will be expected to provide yourself, such as file folders and paper. The policy on textbooks varies from one college to another, but on most courses today students are expected to buy their own. If you look after yours carefully, then you have the option to sell it on to someone else afterwards and recoup some of your money. If you scribble all over it, leave it on the floor and then tread on it, turn back pages and rapidly turn it into a dog-eared, misshapen version of its former self then you miss out on this opportunity.

13

Unfortunately students often squander other opportunities to utilise resources in the best way – usually because they don't think about them very much, if at all. To help, below is a list of the resources you should consider important – with a few tips on how to get the best out of them.

- **Course information** This includes your course specification, this Study Guide and all the other information relating to your BTEC National which you can find on the Edexcel website. Add to this all the information given to you at college relating to your course, including term dates, assignment dates and, of course, your timetable. This should not be 'dead' information that you glance at once and then discard or ignore. Rather it is important reference material that you need to store somewhere obvious, so that you can look at it whenever you have a query or need to clarify something quickly.

- **Course materials** In this group is your textbook (if there is one), the handouts you are given as well as print-outs and notes you make yourself. File handouts the moment you are given them and put them into an A4 folder bought for the purpose. You will need one for each unit you study. Some students prefer lever-arch files but these are more bulky so more difficult to carry around all day. Unless you have a locker at college it can be easier to keep a lever arch file at home for permanent storage of past handouts and notes for a unit and carry an A4 folder with you which contains current topic information. Filing handouts and print-outs promptly means they don't get lost. They are also less likely to get crumpled, torn or tatty becoming virtually unreadable. Unless you have a private and extensive source of income then this is even more important if you have to pay for every print-out you take in your college resource centre. If you are following a course such as Art and Design, then there will be all your art materials and the pieces you produce. You must look after these with great care.

- **Other stationery items** Having your own pens, pencils, notepad, punch, stapler and sets of dividers is essential. Nothing irritates tutors more than watching one punch circulate around a group – except, perhaps, the student who trudges into class with nothing to write on or with. Your dividers should be clearly labelled to help you store and find notes, print-outs and handouts fast. Similarly, your notes should be clearly headed and dated. If you are writing notes up from your own research then you will have to include your source. Researching information is explained in Step 6 – Sharpen your skills.

- **Equipment and facilities** These include your college library and resource centres, the college computer network and other college equipment you can use, such as laptop computers, photocopiers and presentation equipment. Much of this may be freely available; others – such as using the photocopier in the college library or the printers in a resource centre – may cost you money. Many useful resources will be electronic, such as DVDs or electronic journals and databases. At home you may have your own computer with Internet access to count as a resource. Finally, include any specialist equipment and facilities available for your particular course that you use at college or have at home.

Utilise all your resources

14

All centralised college resources and facilities are invaluable if you know how to use them – but can be baffling when you don't. Your induction should have included how to use the library, resource centre(s) and computer network. You should also have been informed of the policy on using IT equipment which determines what you can and can't do when you are using college computers. If, by any chance, you missed this then go and check it out for yourself. Library and resource centre staff will be only too pleased to give you helpful advice – especially if you pick a quiet time to call in. You can also find out about the allowable ways to transfer data between your college computer and your home computer if your options are limited because of IT security.

Having a study buddy is a good idea

■ **People** You are surrounded by people who are valuable resources: your tutor(s), specialist staff at college, your employer and work colleagues, your relatives and any friends who have particular skills or who work in the same area you are studying. Other members of your class are also useful resources – although they may not always seem like it! Use them, for example, to discuss topics out of class time. A good debate between a group of students can often raise and clarify issues that there may not be time to discuss fully in class. Having a study buddy is another good idea – you get/make notes for them when they are away and vice versa. That way you don't miss anything.

If you want information or help from someone, especially anyone outside your immediate circle, then remember to get the basics right! Approach them courteously, do your homework first so that you are well-prepared and remember that you are asking for assistance – not trying to get them to do the work for you! If someone has agreed to allow you to interview them as part of your research for an assignment or project then good preparations will be vital, as you will see in Step 6 – Sharpen your Skills (see page 22).

One word of warning: be wary about using information from friends or relatives who have done a similar or earlier course. First, the slant of the material they were given may be different. It may also be out-of-date. And *never* copy anyone else's written assignments. This is **plagiarism** – a deadly sin in the educational world. You can read more about this in Step 5 – Understand your assessment (see page 16).

■ **You!** You have the ability to be your own best resource or your own worst enemy! The difference depends upon your work skills, your personal skills and your attitude to your course and other people. You have already seen how to use time wisely. Throughout this guide you will find out how to sharpen and improve other work and personal skills and how to get the most out of your course – but it is up to you to read it and apply your new-found knowledge! This is why attributes like a positive attitude, an enquiring mind and the ability to focus on what is important all have a major impact on your final result.

15

PLUSPOINTS

+ Resources help you to achieve your qualification. You will squander these unwittingly if you don't know what they are or how to use them properly.

+ Course information needs to be stored safely for future reference: course materials need to be filed promptly and accurately so that you can find them quickly.

+ You need your own set of key stationery items; you also need to know how to use any central facilities or resources such as the library, learning resource centres and your computer network.

+ People are often a key resource – school or college staff, work colleagues, members of your class, people who are experts in their field.

+ You can be your own best resource! Develop the skills you need to be able to work quickly and accurately and to get the most out of other people who can help you.

ACTION POINTS

✓ Under the same headings as in this section, list all the resources you need for your course and tick off those you currently have. Then decide how and when you can obtain anything vital that you lack.

✓ Check that you know how to access and use all the shared resources to which you have access at school or college.

✓ Pair up with someone on your course as a study buddy – and don't let them down!

✓ Test your own storage systems. How fast can you find notes or print-outs you made yesterday/last week/last month – and what condition are they in?

✓ Find out the IT policy at your school or college and make sure you abide by it.

16

STEP FIVE

UNDERSTAND YOUR ASSESSMENT

The key to doing really, really well on any BTEC National course is to understand exactly what you are expected to do in your assignments – and then to do it! It really is as simple as that. So why is it that some people go wrong?

Obviously you may worry that an assignment may be so difficult that it is beyond you. Actually this is highly unlikely to happen because all your assignments are based on topics you will have already covered thoroughly in class. Therefore, if you have attended regularly – and have clarified any queries or worries you have either in class or during your tutorials – this shouldn't happen. If you have had an unavoidable lengthy absence then you may need to review your progress with your tutor and decide how best to cope with the situation. Otherwise, you should note that the main problems with assignments are usually due to far more mundane pitfalls – such as:

✗ not reading the instructions or the assignment brief properly

✗ not understanding what you are supposed to do

✗ only doing part of the task or answering part of a question

✗ skimping the preparation, the research or the whole thing

✗ not communicating your ideas clearly

✗ guessing answers rather than researching properly

✗ padding out answers with irrelevant information

✗ leaving the work until the last minute and then doing it in a rush

✗ ignoring advice and feedback your tutor has given you.

You can avoid all of these traps by following the guidelines below so that you know exactly what you are doing, prepare well and produce your best work.

The assignment 'brief'

The word 'brief' is just another way of saying 'instructions'. Often, though, a 'brief' (despite its name!) may be rather longer. The brief sets the context for the work, defines what evidence you will need to produce and matches the grading criteria to the tasks. It will also give you a schedule for completing the tasks. For example, a brief may include details of a case study you have to read; research you have to carry out or a task you have to do, as well as questions you have to answer. Or it may give you details about a project or group presentation you have to prepare. The type of assignments you receive will depend partly upon the vocational area you are studying, but you can expect some to be in the form of written assignments. Others are likely to be more practical or project-based, especially if you are doing a very practical subject such as Art and Design, Performing Arts or Sport. You may also be assessed in the workplace. For example, this is a course requirement if you are studying Children's Care, Learning and Development.

The assignment brief may also include the **learning outcomes** to which it relates. These tell you the purpose of the assessment and the knowledge you need to demonstrate to obtain a required grade. If your brief doesn't list the learning outcomes, then you should check this information against the unit specification to see the exact knowledge you need to demonstrate.

The grade(s) you can obtain will also be stated on the assignment brief. Sometimes an assignment will focus on just one grade. Others may give you the opportunity to develop or extend your work to progress to a higher grade. This is often dependent upon submitting acceptable work at the previous grade first. You will see examples of this in the Marked Assignment section of this Study Guide on page 121.

The brief will also tell you if you have to do part of the work as a member of a group. In this case, you must identify your own contribution. You may also be expected to take part in a **peer review**, where you all give feedback on the contribution of one another. Remember that you should do this as objectively and professionally as possible – not just praise everyone madly in the hope that they will do the same for you! In any assignment where there is a group contribution, there is virtually always an individual component, so that your individual grade can be assessed accurately.

Finally, your assignment brief should state the final deadline for handing in the work as well as any interim review dates when you can discuss your progress and ideas with your tutor. These are very important dates indeed and should be entered immediately into your diary or planner. You should schedule your work around these dates so that you have made a start by the first date. This will then enable you to note any queries or significant issues you want to discuss. Otherwise you will waste a valuable opportunity to obtain useful feedback on your progress. Remember, too, to take a notebook to any review meetings so that you can write down the guidance you are given.

Your school or college rules and regulations

Your school or college will have a number of policies and guidelines about assignments and assessment. These will deal with issues such as:

- The procedure you must follow if you have a serious personal problem so cannot meet the deadline date and need an extension.

- Any penalties for missing a deadline date without any good reason.

- The penalties for copying someone else's work (**plagiarism**). These will be severe so make sure that you never share your work (including your CDs) with anyone else and don't ask to borrow theirs.

- The procedure to follow if you are unhappy with the final grade you receive.

Even though it is unlikely that you will ever need to use any of these policies, it is sensible to know they exist, and what they say, just as a safeguard.

Understanding the question or task

There are two aspects to a question or task that need attention. The first are the *command words*, which are explained below. The second are the *presentation instructions*, so that if you are asked to produce a table or graph or report then you do exactly that – and don't write a list or an essay instead!

Command words are used to specify how a question must be answered, eg 'explain', 'describe', 'analyse', 'evaluate'. These words relate to the type of answer required. So whereas you may be asked to 'describe' something at Pass level, you will need to do more (such as 'analyse' or 'evaluate') to achieve Merit or Distinction grade.

Many students fail to get a higher grade because they do not realise the difference between these words. They simply don't know *how* to analyse or evaluate, so give an explanation instead. Just adding to a list or giving a few more details will never give you a higher grade – instead you need to change your whole approach to the answer.

The **grading grid** for each unit of your course gives you the command words, so that you can find out exactly what you have to do in each unit, to obtain a Pass, Merit and Distinction. The following charts show you what is usually required when you see a particular command word. You can use this, and the marked assignments on pages 121–168, to see the difference between the types of answers required for each grade. (The assignments your centre gives you will be specially written to ensure you have the opportunity to achieve all the possible grades.) Remember, though, that these are just examples to guide you. The exact response will often depend upon the way a question is worded, so if you have any doubts at all check with your tutor before you start work.

There are two other important points to note:

- Sometimes the same command word may be repeated for different grades – such as 'create' or 'explain'. In this case the *complexity* or *range* of the task itself increases at the higher grades – as you will see if you read the grading grid for the unit.

- Command words can also vary depending upon your vocational area. If you are studying Performing Arts or Art and Design you will probably find several command words that an Engineer or IT Practitioner would not – and vice versa!

To obtain a Pass grade

To achieve this grade you must usually demonstrate that you understand the important facts relating to a topic and can state these clearly and concisely.

Command word	What this means
Create (or produce)	Make, invent or construct an item.
Describe	Give a clear, straightforward description that includes all the main points and links these together logically.
Define	Clearly explain what a particular term means and give an example, if appropriate, to show what you mean.
Explain . . . how/why	Set out in detail the meaning of something, with reasons. It is often helpful to give an example of what you mean. Start with the topic then give the 'how' or 'why'.
Identify	Distinguish and state the main features or basic facts relating to a topic.
Interpret	Define or explain the meaning of something.
Illustrate	Give examples to show what you mean.
List	Provide the information required in a list rather than in continuous writing.
Outline	Write a clear description that includes all the main points but avoid going into too much detail.
Plan (or devise)	Work out and explain how you would carry out a task or activity.
Select (and present) information	Identify relevant information to support the argument you are making and communicate this in an appropriate way.
State	Write a clear and full account.
Undertake	Carry out a specific activity.
Examples: **Identify** the main features on a digital camera. **Describe** your usual lifestyle. **Outline** the steps to take to carry out research for an assignment.	

19

To obtain a Merit grade

To obtain this grade you must prove that you can apply your knowledge in a specific way.

Command word	What this means
Analyse	Identify separate factors, say how they are related and how each one relates to the topic.
Classify	Sort your information into appropriate categories before presenting or explaining it.
Compare and contrast	Identify the main factors that apply in two or more situations and explain the similarities and differences or advantages and disadvantages.
Demonstrate	Provide several relevant examples or appropriate evidence which support the arguments you are making. In some vocational areas this may also mean giving a practical performance.
Discuss	Provide a thoughtful and logical argument to support the case you are making.
Explain (in detail)	Provide details and give reasons and/or evidence to clearly support the argument you are making.
Implement	Put into practice or operation. You may also have to interpret or justify the effect or result.
Interpret	Understand and explain an effect or result.
Justify	Give appropriate reasons to support your opinion or views and show how you arrived at these conclusions.
Relate/report	Give a full account of, with reasons.
Research	Carry out a full investigation.
Specify	Provide full details and descriptions of selected items or activities.
Examples: **Compare and contrast** the performance of two different digital cameras. **Justify** your usual lifestyle. **Explain in detail** the steps to take to research an assignment.	

To obtain a Distinction grade

To obtain this grade you must prove that you can make a reasoned judgement based on appropriate evidence.

Command word	What this means
Analyse	Identify the key factors, show how they are linked and explain the importance and relevance of each.
Assess	Give careful consideration to all the factors or events that apply and identify which are the most important and relevant with reasons for your views.
Comprehensively explain	Give a very detailed explanation that covers all the relevant points and give reasons for your views or actions.
Comment critically	Give your view after you have considered all the evidence, particularly the importance of both the relevant positive and negative aspects.
Evaluate	Review the information and then bring it together to form a conclusion. Give evidence to support each of your views or statements.
Evaluate critically	Review the information to decide the degree to which something is true, important or valuable. Then assess possible alternatives taking into account their strengths and weaknesses if they were applied instead. Then give a precise and detailed account to explain your opinion.
Summarise	Identify review the main, relevant factors and/or arguments so that these are explained in a clear and concise manner.
Examples: **Assess** ten features commonly found on a digital camera. **Evaluate critically** your usual lifestyle. **Analyse** your own ability to carry out effective research for an assignment.	

Responding positively

This is often the most important attribute of all! If you believe that assignments give you the opportunity to demonstrate what you know and how you can apply it *and* positively respond to the challenge by being determined to give it your best shot, then you will do far better than someone who is defeated before they start.

It obviously helps, too, if you are well organised and have confidence in your own abilities – which is what the next section is all about!

PLUSPOINTS

+ Many mistakes in assignments are through errors that can easily be avoided such as not reading the instructions properly or doing only part of the task that was set!

+ Always read the assignment brief very carefully indeed. Check that you understand exactly what you have to do and the learning outcomes you must demonstrate.

+ Make a note of the deadline for an assignment and any interim review dates on your planner. Schedule work around these dates so that you can make the most of reviews with your tutor.

+ Make sure you know about school or college policies relating to assessment, such as how to obtain an extension or query a final grade.

+ For every assignment, make sure you understand the command words, which tell you how to answer the question, and the presentation instructions, which say what you must produce.

+ Command words are shown in the grading grid for each unit of your qualification. Expect command words and/or the complexity of a task to be different at higher grades, because you have to demonstrate higher-level skills.

ACTION POINTS

✓ Discuss with your tutor the format (style) of assignments you are likely to receive on your course, eg assignments, projects, or practical work where you are observed.

✓ Check the format of the assignments in the Marked Assignments section of this book. Look at the type of work students did to gain a Pass and then look at the difference in the Merit answers. Read the tutor's comments carefully and ask your own tutor if there is anything you do not understand.

✓ Check out all the policies and guidelines at your school or college that relate to assessment and make sure you understand them.

✓ Check out the grading grid for the units you are currently studying and identify the command words for each grade. Then check you understand what they mean using the explanations above. If there are any words that are not included, ask your tutor to explain the meanings and what you would be required to do.

STEP SIX

SHARPEN YOUR SKILLS

To do your best in any assignment you need a number of skills. Some of these may be vocationally specific, or professional, skills that you are learning as part of your course – such as acting or dancing if you are taking a Performing Arts course or, perhaps, football if you are following a Sports course. Others, though, are broader skills that will help you to do well in assignments no matter what subjects or topics you are studying – such as communicating clearly and cooperating with others.

Some of these skills you will have already and in some areas you may be extremely proficient. Knowing where your weaknesses lie, though, and doing something about them has many benefits. You will work more quickly, more accurately *and* have increased confidence in your own abilities. As an extra bonus, all these skills also make you more effective at work – so there really is no excuse for not giving yourself a quick skills check and then remedying any problem areas.

This section contains hints and tips to help you check out and improve each of the following areas:

- Your numeracy skills
- Keyboarding and document preparation
- Your IT skills
- Your written communication skills
- Working with others
- Researching information
- Making a presentation
- Problem solving and staying focused

Improving your numeracy skills

Some people have the idea that they can ignore numeracy because this skill isn't relevant to their vocational area – such as Art and Design or Children's Care, Learning and Development. If this is how you think then you are wrong! Numeracy is a life skill that everyone needs, so if you can't carry out basic calculations accurately then you will have problems, often when you least expect them.

Fortunately there are several things you can do to remedy this situation:

- Practise basic calculations in your head and then check them on a calculator.
- Ask your tutor if there are any essential calculations which give you difficulties.
- Use your onscreen calculator (or a spreadsheet package) to do calculations for you when you are using your computer.
- Try your hand at Sudoku puzzles – either on paper or by using a software package or online at sites such as www.websudoku.com/.
- Investigate puzzle sites and brain training software, such as http://school.discovery.com/brainboosters/ and Dr Kawashima's Brain Training by Nintendo.
- Check out online sites such as www.bbc.co.uk/skillswise/ and www.bbc.co.uk/schools/ks3bitesize/maths/number/index.shtml to improve your skills.

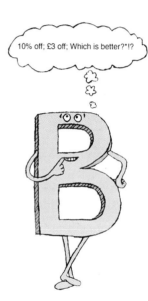

Numeracy is a life skill

Keyboarding and document preparation

- Think seriously about learning to touch type to save hours of time! Your school or college may have a workshop you can join or you can learn online such as by downloading a free program at www.sense-lang.org/typing/ or practising on sites such as www.computerlab.kids.new.net/keyboarding.htm.
- Obtain correct examples of document formats you will have to use, such as a report or summary. Your tutor may provide you with these or you can find examples in many communication textbooks.
- Proof-read work you produce on a computer *carefully*. Remember that your spell checker will not pick up every mistake you make, such as a mistyped word that makes another word (eg form/from; sheer/shear)

and grammar checkers, too, are not without their problems! This means you still have to read your work through yourself. If possible, let your work go 'cold' before you do this so that you read it afresh and don't make assumptions about what you have written. Then read word by word to make sure it still makes sense and there are no silly mistakes, such as missing or duplicated words.

- Make sure your work looks professional by using an appropriate typeface and font size as well as suitable margins.
- Print out your work carefully and store it neatly, so it looks in pristine condition when you hand it in.

Your IT skills

- Check that you can use the main features of all the software packages that you will need to produce your assignments, such as Word, Excel and PowerPoint.
- Adopt a good search engine, such as Google, and learn to use it properly. Many have online tutorials such as www.googleguide.com.
- Develop your IT skills to enable you to enhance your assignments appropriately. For example, this may include learning how to import and export text and artwork from one package to another; taking digital photographs and inserting them into your work and/or creating drawings or diagrams by using appropriate software for your course.

Your written communication skills

A poor vocabulary will reduce your ability to explain yourself clearly; work peppered with spelling or punctuation errors looks unprofessional.

- Read more. This introduces you to new words and familiarises you over and over again with the correct way to spell words.
- Look up words you don't understand in a dictionary and then try to use them yourself in conversation.
- Use the Thesaurus in Word to find alternatives to words you find yourself regularly repeating, to add variety to your work.
- *Never* use words you don't understand in the hope that they sound impressive!
- Do crosswords to improve your word power and spelling.
- Resolve to master punctuation – especially apostrophes – either by using an online programme or working your way through the relevant section of a communication textbook that you like.
- Check out online sites such as www.bbc.co.uk/skillswise/ and www.bbc.co.uk/schools/gcsebitesize/english/ as well as puzzle sites with communication questions such as http://school.discovery.com/brainboosters/.

Working with others

In your private life you can choose who you want to be with and how you respond to them. At work you cannot do that – you are paid to be professional and this means working alongside a wide variety of people, some of whom you may like and some of whom you may not!

The same applies at school or college. By the time you have reached BTEC National level you will be expected to have outgrown wanting to work with your best friends on every project! You may not be very keen on everyone who is in the same team as you, but – at the very least – you can be pleasant, cooperative and helpful. In a large group this isn't normally too difficult. You may find it much harder if you have to partner someone who has very different ideas and ways of working to you.

In this case it may help if you:

- Realise that everyone is different and that your ways of working may not always be the best!
- Are prepared to listen and contribute to a discussion (positively) in equal amounts. Make sure, too, that you encourage the quiet members of the group to speak up by asking them what their views are. The ability to draw other people into the discussion is an important and valuable skill to learn.
- Write down what you have said you will do, so that you don't forget anything.
- Are prepared to do your fair share of the work.
- Discuss options and alternatives with people – don't give them orders or meekly accept instructions and then resent it afterwards.
- Don't expect other people to do what you wouldn't be prepared to do.
- Are sensitive to other people's feelings and remember that they may have personal problems or issues that affect their behaviour.
- *Always* keep your promises and never let anyone down when they are depending upon you.
- Don't flounce around or lose your temper if things get tough. Instead take a break while you cool down. Then sit down and discuss the issues that are annoying you.
- Help other people to reach a compromise when necessary, by acting as peacemaker.

Researching information

Poor researchers either cannot find what they want or find too much – and then drown in a pile of papers. If you find yourself drifting aimlessly around a library when you want information or printing out dozens of pages for no apparent purpose, then this section is for you!

- Always check *exactly* what it is you need to find and how much detail is needed. Write down a few key words to keep yourself focused.
- Discipline yourself to ignore anything that is irrelevant – from books with interesting titles to websites which sound tempting but have little to do with your topic or key words.
- Remember that you could theoretically research information forever! So at some time you have to call a halt. Learning when to do this is another skill, but you can learn this by writing out a schedule which clearly states when you have to stop looking and start sorting out your information and writing about it!

- In a library, check you know how the books are stored and what other types of media are available. If you can't find what you are looking for then ask the librarian for help. Checking the index in a book is the quickest way to find out whether it contains information related to your key words. Put it back if it doesn't or if you can't understand it. If you find three or four books and/or journals that contain what you need then that is usually enough.

- Online use a good search engine and use the summary of the search results to check out the best sites. Force yourself to check out sites beyond page one of the search results! When you enter a site investigate it carefully – use the site map if necessary. It isn't always easy to find exactly what you want. Bookmark sites you find helpful and will want to use again and only take print-outs when the information is closely related to your key words.

- Talk to people who can help you (see also Step 4 – Utilise all your resources) and prepare in advance by thinking about the best questions to ask. Always explain why you want the information and don't expect anyone to tell you anything that is confidential or sensitive – such as personal information or financial details. Always write clear notes so that you remember what you have been told, by whom and when. If you are wise you will also note down their contact details so that you can contact them again if you think of anything later. If you remember to be courteous and thank them for their help, this shouldn't be a problem.

- Store all your precious information carefully and neatly in a labelled folder so that you can find it easily. Then, when you are ready to start work, reread it and extract that which is most closely related to your key words and the task you are doing.

- Make sure you state the source of all the information you quote by including the name of the author or the web address, either in the text or as part of a bibliography at the end. Your school or college will have a help sheet which will tell you exactly how to do this.

Making a presentation

This involves several skills – which is why it is such a popular way of finding out what students can do! It will test your ability to work in a team, speak in public and use IT (normally PowerPoint) – as well as your nerves. It is therefore excellent practice for many of the tasks you will have to do when you are at work – from attending an interview to talking to an important client.

You will be less nervous if you have prepared well and have rehearsed your role beforehand. You will produce a better, more professional presentation if you take note of the following points.

- If you are working as a team, work out everyone's strengths and weaknesses and divide up the work (fairly) taking these into account. Work out, too, how long each person should speak and who would be the best as the 'leader' who introduces each person and then summarises everything at the end.

PLUSPOINTS

+ Poor numeracy skills can let you down in your assignments and at work. Work at improving these if you regularly struggle with even simple calculations.

+ Good keyboarding, document production and IT skills can save you hours of time and mean that your work is of a far more professional standard. Improve any of these areas which are letting you down.

+ Your written communication skills will be tested in many assignments. Work at improving areas of weakness, such as spelling, punctuation or vocabulary.

+ You will be expected to work cooperatively with other people both at work and during many assignments. Be sensitive to other people's feelings, not just your own, and always be prepared to do your fair share of the work and help other people when you can.

+ To research effectively you need to know exactly what you are trying to find and where to look. This means understanding how reference media is stored in your library as well as how to search online. Good organisation skills also help so that you store important information carefully and can find it later. And never forget to include your sources in a bibliography.

+ Making a presentation requires several skills and may be nerve-racking at first. You will reduce your problems if you prepare well, are not too ambitious and have several run-throughs beforehand. Remember to speak clearly and a little more slowly than normal and smile from time to time!

ACTION POINTS

✓ Test both your numeracy and literacy skills at http://www.move-on.org.uk/testyourskills.asp# to check your current level. You don't need to register on the site if you click to do the 'mini-test' instead. If either need improvement, get help at http://www.bbc.co.uk/keyskills/it/1.shtml.

✓ Do the following two tasks with a partner to jerk your brain into action!

- Each write down 36 simple calculations in a list, eg 8 x 6, 19 – 8, 14 + 6. Then exchange lists. See who can answer the most correctly in the shortest time.

- Each write down 30 short random words (no more than 8 letters), eg cave, table, happily. Exchange lists. You each have three minutes to try to remember as many words as possible. Then hand back the list and write down all those you can recall. See who can remember the most.

✓ Assess your own keyboarding, proof-reading, document production, written communication and IT skills. Then find out if your tutors agree with you!

✓ List ten traits in other people that drive you mad. Then, for each one, suggest what you could do to cope with the problem (or solve it) rather than make a fuss. Compare your ideas with other members of your group.

✓ Take a note of all feedback you receive from your tutors, especially in relation to working with other people, researching and giving presentations. In each case focus on their suggestions and ideas so that you continually improve your skills throughout the course.

27

■ Don't be over-ambitious. Take account of your time-scale, resources and the skills of the team. Remember that a simple, clear presentation is often more professional than an over-elaborate or complicated one where half the visual aids don't work properly!

■ If you are using PowerPoint try to avoid preparing every slide with bullet points! For variety, include some artwork and vary the designs. Remember that you should *never* just read your slides to the audience! Instead prepare notes that you can print out that will enable you to enhance and extend what the audience is reading.

- Your preparations should also include checking the venue and time; deciding what to wear and getting it ready; preparing, checking and printing any handouts; deciding what questions might be asked and how to answer these.

- Have several run-throughs beforehand and check your timings. Check, too, that you can be heard clearly. This means lifting up your head and 'speaking' to the back of the room a little more slowly and loudly than you normally do.

- On the day, arrive in plenty of time so that you aren't rushed or stressed. Remember that taking deep breaths helps to calm your nerves.

- Start by introducing yourself clearly and smile at the audience. If it helps, find a friendly face and pretend you are just talking to that person.

- Answer any questions honestly and don't exaggerate, guess or waffle. If you don't know the answer then say so!

- If you are giving the presentation in a team, help out someone else who is struggling with a question if you know the answer.

- Don't get annoyed or upset if you get any negative feedback afterwards. Instead take note so that you can concentrate on improving your own performance next time. And don't focus on one or two criticisms and ignore all the praise you received! Building on the good and minimising the bad is how everyone improves in life!

STEP SEVEN

MAXIMISE YOUR OPPORTUNITIES AND MANAGE YOUR PROBLEMS

Like most things in life, you may have a few ups and downs on your course – particularly if you are studying over quite a long time, such as one or two years. Sometimes everything will be marvellous – you are enjoying all the units, you are up-to-date with your work, you are finding the subjects interesting and having no problems with any of your research tasks. At other times you may struggle a little more. You may find one or two topics rather tedious, or there may be distractions or worries in your personal life that you have to cope with. You may struggle to concentrate on the work and do your best.

Rather than just suffering in silence or gritting your teeth if things go a bit awry it is sensible if you have an action plan to help you cope. Equally, rather than just accepting good opportunities for additional experiences or learning, it is also wise to plan how to make the best of these. This section will show you how to do this.

Making the most of your opportunities

The following are examples of opportunities to find out more about information relevant to your course or to try putting some of your skills into practice.

- **External visits** You may go out of college on visits to different places or organisations. These are not days off – there is a reason for making each trip. Prepare in advance by reading around relevant topics and make notes of useful information whilst you are there. Then write (or type) it up neatly as soon as you can and file it where you can find it again!

- **Visiting speakers** Again, people are asked to talk to your group for a purpose. You are likely to be asked to contribute towards questions that may be asked – which may be submitted in advance so that the speaker is clear on the topics you are studying. Think carefully about information that you would find helpful so that you can ask one or two relevant and useful questions. Take notes whilst the speaker is addressing your group, unless someone is recording the session. Be prepared to thank the speaker on behalf of your group if you are asked to do so.

- **Professional contacts** These will be the people you meet on work experience doing the real job that one day you hope to do. Make the most of meeting these people to find out about the vocational area of your choice.

- **Work experience** If you need to undertake practical work for any particular units of your BTEC National qualification, and if you are studying full-time, then your tutor will organise a work experience placement for you and talk to you about the evidence you need to obtain. You may also be issued with a special log book or diary in which to record your experiences. Before you start your placement, check that you are clear about all the details, such as the time you will start and leave, the name of your supervisor, what you should wear and what you should do if you are ill during the placement and cannot attend. Read and reread the units to which your evidence will apply and make sure you understand the grading criteria and what you need to obtain. Then make a note of appropriate headings to record your information. Try to make time to write up your notes, log book and/or diary every night, whilst your experiences are fresh in your mind.

- **In your own workplace** You may be studying your BTEC National qualification on a part-time basis and also have a full-time job in the same vocational area. Or you may be studying full-time and have a part-time job just to earn some money. In either case you should be alert to opportunities to find out more about topics that relate to your workplace, no matter how generally. For example, many BTEC courses include topics such as health and safety, teamwork, dealing with customers, IT security and communications – to name but a few. All these are topics that your employer will have had to address and finding out more about these will broaden your knowledge and help to give more depth to your assignment responses.

- **Television programmes, newspapers, Podcasts and other information sources.** No matter what vocational area you are studying, the media are likely to be an invaluable source of information. You should be alert to any news bulletins that relate to your studies as well as relevant information in more topical television programmes. For example, if you are studying Art and Design then you should make a particular effort to watch the *Culture Show* as well as programmes on artists, exhibitions or other topics of interest. Business students should find inspiration by watching *Dragons Den*, *The Apprentice* and the *Money Programme* and Travel and Tourism students should watch holiday, travel and adventure programmes. If you are studying Media, Music and Performing Arts then you are spoiled for choice! Whatever your vocational choice, there will be television and radio programmes of special interest to you.

Remember that you can record television programmes to watch later if you prefer, and check out newspaper headlines online and from sites such as BBC news. The same applies to Podcasts. Of course, to know which information is relevant means that you must be familiar with the content of all the units you are studying, so it is useful to know what topics you will be learning about in the months to come, as well as the ones you are covering now. That way you can recognise useful opportunities when they arise.

The media are invaluable sources of information

Minimising problems

If you are fortunate, any problems you experience on your course will only be minor ones. For example, you may struggle to keep yourself motivated every single day and there may be times that you are having difficulty with a topic. Or you may be struggling to work with someone else in your team or to understand a particular tutor.

During induction you should have been told which tutor to talk to in this situation, and who to see if that person is absent or if you would prefer to see someone else. If you are having difficulties which are distracting you and affecting your work then it is sensible to ask to see your tutor promptly so that you can talk in confidence, rather than just trusting to luck everything will go right again. It is a rare student who is madly enthusiastic about every part of a course and all the other people on the course, so your tutor won't be surprised and will be able to give you useful guidance to help you stay on track.

If you are very unlucky, you may have a more serious personal problem to deal with. In this case it is important that you know the main sources of help in your school or college and how to access these.

- **Professional counselling** There may be a professional counselling service if you have a concern that you don't want to discuss with any teaching staff. If you book an appointment to see a counsellor then you can be certain that nothing you say will ever be mentioned to another member of staff without your permission.

- **Student complaint procedures** If you have a serious complaint to make then the first step is to talk to a tutor, but you should be aware of the formal student complaint procedures that exist if you cannot resolve the problem informally. Note that these are only used for serious issues, not for minor difficulties.

- **Student appeals procedures** If you cannot agree with a tutor about a final grade for an assignment then you need to check the grading criteria and ask the tutor to explain how the grade was awarded. If you are still unhappy then you should see your personal tutor. If you still disagree then you have the right to make a formal appeal.

- **Student disciplinary procedures** These exist so that all students who flout the rules in a school or college will be dealt with in the same way. Obviously it is wise to avoid getting into trouble at any time, but if you find yourself on the wrong side of the regulations do read the procedures carefully to see what could happen. Remember that being honest about what happened and making a swift apology is always the wisest course of action, rather than being devious or trying to blame someone else.

- **Serious illness** Whether this affects you or a close family member, it could severely affect your attendance. The sooner you discuss the problem with your tutor the better. This is because you will be missing notes and information from the first day you do not attend. Many students under-estimate the ability of their tutors to find inventive solutions in this type of situation – from sending notes by post to updating you electronically if you are well enough to cope with the work.

PLUSPOINTS

+ Some students miss out on opportunities to learn more about relevant topics. This may be because they haven't read the unit specifications, so don't know what topics they will be learning about in future; haven't prepared in advance or don't take advantage of occasions when they can listen to an expert and perhaps ask questions. Examples of these occasions include external visits, visiting speakers, work experience, being at work and watching television.

+ Many students encounter minor difficulties, especially if their course lasts a year or two. It is important to talk to your tutor, or another appropriate person, promptly if you have a worry that is affecting your work.

+ All schools and colleges have procedures for dealing with important issues and problems such as serious complaints, major illnesses, student appeals and disciplinary matters. It is important to know what these are.

ACTION POINTS

✓ List the type of opportunities available on your course for obtaining more information and talking to experts. Then check with your tutor to make sure you haven't missed out any.

✓ Check out the content of each unit you will be studying so that you know the main topics you have still to study.

✓ Identify the type of information you can find on television, in newspapers and in Podcasts that will be relevant to your studies.

✓ Check out your school or college documents and procedures to make sure that you know who to talk to in a crisis and who you can see if the first person is absent.

✓ Find out where you can read a copy of the main procedures in your school or college that might affect you if you have a serious problem. Then do so.

AND FINALLY . . .

Don't expect this Introduction to be of much use if you skim through it quickly and then put it to one side. Instead, refer to it whenever you need to remind yourself about something related to your course.

The same applies to the rest of this Student Guide. The Activities in the next section have been written to help you to demonstrate your understanding of many of the key topics contained in the core or specialist units you are studying. Your tutor may tell you to do these at certain times; otherwise there is nothing to stop you working through them yourself!

Similarly, the Marked Assignments in the final section have been written to show you how your assignments may be worded. You can also see the type of response that will achieve a Pass, Merit and Distinction – as well as the type of response that won't! Read these carefully and if any comment or grade puzzles you, ask your tutor to explain it.

Then keep this guide in a safe place so that you can use it whenever you need to refresh your memory. That way, you will get the very best out of your course – and yourself!

GLOSSARY

Note: all words highlighted in bold in the text are defined in the glossary.

Accreditation of Prior Learning (APL)

APL is an assessment process that enables your previous achievements and experiences to count towards your qualification providing your evidence is authentic, current, relevant and sufficient.

Apprenticeships

Schemes that enable you to work and earn money at the same time as you gain further qualifications (an **NVQ** award and a technical certificate) and improve your key skills. Apprentices learn work-based skills relevant to their job role and their chosen industry. You can find out more at www.apprenticeships.org.uk/

Assessment methods

Methods, such as **assignments**, case studies and practical tasks, used to check that your work demonstrates the learning and understanding required for your qualification.

Assessor

The tutor who marks or assesses your work.

Assignment

A complex task or mini-project set to meet specific **grading criteria**.

Awarding body

The organisation which is responsible for devising, assessing and issuing qualifications. The awarding body for all BTEC qualifications is Edexcel.

Core units

On a BTEC National course these are the compulsory or mandatory units that all students must complete to gain the qualification. Some BTEC qualifications have an over-arching title, eg Engineering, but within Engineering you can choose different routes. In this case you will study both common core units that are common to all engineering qualifications and **specialist core unit(s)** which are specific to your chosen **pathway**.

Degrees

These are higher education qualifications which are offered by universities and colleges. Foundation degrees take two years to complete; honours degrees may take three years or longer. See also **Higher National Certificates and Diplomas**.

DfES

The Department for Education and Skills: this is the government department responsible for education issues. You can find out more at www.dfes.gov.uk

Distance learning

This enables you to learn and/or study for a qualification without attending an Edexcel centre although you would normally be supported by a member of staff who works there. You communicate with your tutor and/or the centre that organises the distance learning programme by post, telephone or electronically.

Educational Maintenance Award (EMA)

This is a means-tested award which provides eligible students under 19, who are studying a full-time course at school or college, with a cash sum of money every week. See http://www.dfes.gov.uk/financialhelp/ema/ for up-to-date details.

External verification

Formal checking by a representative of Edexcel of the way a BTEC course is delivered. This includes sampling various assessments to check content and grading.

Final major project

This is a major, individual piece of work that is designed to enable you to demonstrate you have achieved several learning outcomes for a BTEC National qualification in the creative or performing arts. Like all assessments, this is internally assessed.

Forbidden combinations

Qualifications or units that cannot be taken simultaneously because their content is too similar.

GLH

See **Guided Learning Hours** on page 34

Grade

The rating (Pass, Merit or Distinction) given to the mark you have obtained which identifies the standard you have achieved.

Grade boundaries

The pre-set points at which the total points you have earned for different units converts to the overall grade(s) for your qualification.

Grading criteria

The standard you have to demonstrate to obtain a particular grade in the unit, in other words, what you have to prove you can do.

Grading domains

The main areas of learning which support the **learning outcomes**. On a BTEC National course these are: application of knowledge and understanding; development of practical and technical skills; personal development for occupational roles; application of generic and **key skills**. Generic skills are basic skills needed wherever you work, such as the ability to work cooperatively as a member of a team.

Grading grid

The table in each unit of your BTEC qualification specification that sets out the **grading criteria**.

Guided Learning Hours (GLH)

The approximate time taken to deliver a unit which includes the time taken for direct teaching, instruction and assessment and for you to carry out directed assignments or directed individual study. It does not include any time you spend on private study or researching an assignment. The GLH determines the size of the unit. At BTEC National level, units are either 30, 60, 90 or 120 guided learning hours. By looking at the number of GLH a unit takes, you can see the size of the unit and how long it is likely to take you to learn and understand the topics it contains.

Higher education (HE)

Post-secondary and post-further education, usually provided by universities and colleges.

Higher level skills

Skills such as evaluating or critically assessing complex information that are more difficult than lower level skills such as writing a description or making out a list. You must be able to demonstrate higher level skills to achieve a Distinction grade.

Higher National Certificates and Diplomas

Higher National Certificates and Diplomas are vocational qualifications offered at colleges around the country. Certificates are part-time and designed to be studied by people who are already in work; students can use their work experiences to build on their learning. Diplomas are full-time courses – although often students will spend a whole year on work experience part way through their Diploma. Higher Nationals are roughly equivalent to half a degree.

Indicative reading

Recommended books and journals whose content is both suitable and relevant for the unit.

Induction

A short programme of events at the start of a course designed to give you essential information and introduce you to your fellow students and tutors so that you can settle down as quickly and easily as possible.

Internal verification

The quality checks carried out by nominated tutor(s) at your school or college to ensure that all assignments are at the right level and cover appropriate learning outcomes. The checks also ensure that all **assessors** are marking work consistently and to the same standard.

Investors in People (IIP)

A national quality standard which sets a level of good practice for the training and development of people. Organisations must demonstrate their commitment to achieve the standard.

Key skills

The transferable, essential skills you need both at work and to run your own life successfully. They are: literacy, numeracy, IT, problem solving, working with others and self-management.

Learning outcomes

The knowledge and skills you must demonstrate to show that you have effectively learned a unit.

Learning support

Additional help that is available to all students in a school or college who have learning difficulties or other special needs. These include reasonable adjustments to help to reduce the effect of a disability or difficulty that would place a student at a substantial disadvantage in an assessment situation.

Levels of study

The depth, breadth and complexity of knowledge, understanding and skills required to achieve a qualification determines its level. Level 2 is broadly equivalent to GCSE level (grades A*-C) and level 3 equates to GCE level. As you successfully achieve one level, you can then progress on to the next. BTEC qualifications are offered at Entry level, then levels 1, 2, 3, 4 and 5.

Learning and Skills Council (LSC)

The government body responsible for planning and funding education and training for everyone aged over 16 in England – except university students. You can find out more at www.lsc.gov.uk

Local Education Authority (LEA)

The local government body responsible for providing education for students of compulsory school age in your area.

Mentor

A more experienced person who will guide and counsel you if you have a problem or difficulty.

Mode of delivery

The way in which a qualification is offered to students, eg part-time, full-time, as a short course or by **distance learning**.

National Occupational Standard (NOS)

These are statements of the skills, knowledge and understanding you need to develop to be competent at a particular job. These are drawn up by the **Sector Skills Councils**.

National Qualification Framework (NQF)

The framework into which all accredited qualifications in the UK are placed. Each is awarded a level based on their difficulty which ensures that all those at the same level are of the same standard. (See also **levels of study**.)

National Vocational Qualification (NVQ)

Qualifications which concentrate upon the practical skills and knowledge required to do a job competently. They are usually assessed in the workplace and range from level 1 (the lowest) to level 5 (the highest).

Nested qualifications

Qualifications which have 'common' units, so that students can easily progress from one to another by adding on more units, such as the BTEC Award, BTEC Certificate and BTEC Diploma.

Pathway

All BTEC National qualifications are comprised of a small number of core units and a larger number of specialist units. These specialist units are grouped into different combinations to provide alternative pathways to achieving the qualification, linked to different career preferences.

Peer review

An occasion when you give feedback on the performance of other members in your team and they, in turn, comment on your performance.

Plagiarism

The practice of copying someone else's work and passing it off as your own. *This is strictly forbidden on all courses.*

Portfolio

A collection of work compiled by a student, usually as evidence of learning to produce for an **assessor**.

Professional body

An organisation that exists to promote or support a particular profession, such as the Law Society and the Royal Institute of British Architects.

Professional development and training

Activities that you can undertake, relevant to your job, that will increase and/or update your knowledge and skills.

Project

A comprehensive piece of work which normally involves original research and investigation either by an individual or a team. The findings and results may be presented in writing and summarised in a presentation.

Qualifications and Curriculum Authority (QCA)

The public body, sponsored by the **DfES**, responsible for maintaining and developing the national curriculum and associated assessments, tests and examinations. It also accredits and monitors qualifications in colleges and at work. You can find out more at www.qca.gov.uk

Quality assurance

In education, this is the process of continually checking that a course of study is meeting the specific requirements set down by the awarding body.

Sector Skills Councils (SSCs)

The 25 employer-led, independent organisations that are responsible for improving workforce skills in the UK by identifying skill gaps and improving learning in the workplace. Each council covers a different type of industry and develops its **National Occupational Standards**.

Semester

Many universities and colleges divide their academic year into two halves or semesters, one from September to January and one from February to July.

Seminar

A learning event between a group of students and a tutor. This may be student-led, following research into a topic which has been introduced earlier.

Specialist core units

See under **Core units**.

Study buddy

A person in your group or class who takes notes for you and keeps you informed of important developments if you are absent. You do the same in return.

Time-constrained assignment

An assessment you must complete within a fixed time limit.

Tutorial

An individual or small group meeting with your tutor at which you can discuss the work you are currently doing and other more general course issues. At an individual tutorial your progress on the course will be discussed and you can also raise any concerns or personal worries you have.

The University and Colleges Admissions Service (UCAS)

The central organisation which processes all applications for higher education courses. You pronounce this 'You-Cass'.

UCAS points

The number of points allocated by **UCAS** for the qualifications you have obtained. **HE** institutions specify how many points you need to be accepted on the courses they offer. You can find out more at www.ucas.com

Unit abstract

The summary at the start of each BTEC unit that tells you what the unit is about.

Unit content

Details about the topics covered by the unit and the knowledge and skills you need to complete it.

Unit points

The number of points you have gained when you complete a unit. These depend upon the grade you achieve (Pass, Merit or Distinction) and the size of the unit as determined by its **guided learning hours**.

Vocational qualification

A qualification which is designed to develop the specific knowledge and understanding relevant to a chosen area of work.

Work experience

Any time you spend on an employer's premises when you carry out work-based tasks as an employee but also learn about the enterprise and develop your skills and knowledge.

ACTIVITIES

39

In this section we are focusing on P3, P4, M3 from Unit 1 – 'Government, Policies and the Public Services'.

For P3 we will be looking at the various government departments and the specific responsibilities they have for uniformed public services in the UK.

We will also consider how uniformed public services are held accountable to all levels of government (central, devolved, regional and local) and to parliament overall.

Examples of the regulatory bodies (such as Inspectorates) that ensure standards are maintained will be examined.

Finally, the mechanisms by which the uniformed public services are accountable to the general public whom they serve (both locally and nationally) are also of great importance.

For P4 and M5 we will be investigating the way government policy is conceived, developed, moves from proposals to Acts of Parliament and is implemented.

The parliamentary process will be examined as will the consultation processes with the public (individuals, pressure groups and businesses).

This area of study is dynamic (ie it is constantly changing), so although text books are useful references, researching the current situation via websites (in particular government and parliamentary websites) is vital to ensure your information and findings are correct.

Content

2) **Know the responsibilities government departments and other levels of government have for specific public services**

The government departments' responsibilities for the uniformed public services: Ministry of Defence; Home Office; Department of Communities and Local Government; HM Revenue and Customs; Department of Health

The roles of individuals and responsibilities to the uniformed public services: Prime Minister (PM); deputy PM; government ministers, eg Home Secretary, Foreign Secretary, ministers; civil servants; county councillors; district councillors; the mayoral role

Accountability of uniformed public services: the inspectorates used to monitor public service activities, eg HM inspectorates (constabularies, prisons, probation, Independent Police Complaints Commission, health care commission, defence vetting agency); local organisations, eg police authorities, health authorities, fire and rescue authorities; how public services are accountable, eg documents including annual reports, objectives, mission statements, internal complaints procedures, management procedures.

3) **Know the processes involved in developing government policies**

Development processes: meetings that will occur to create policies, eg Cabinet meetings, parliamentary committees and subcommittees, the use of White Papers and Green Papers in parliament, consultation meetings, public meetings or enquiries; representations from outside government

The legal processes used to create legislation: the drafting of the statute; laying before parliament; parliamentary readings; voting in House of Commons and Lords; signature by the monarch; setting dates of implementation; issuing guidance and directives to public services to support the implementation and identify their accountability; advertisements in media to publicise the law; financing of charities and organisations to assist in the implementation of policies.

Grading criteria

P3 describe three government departments and their responsibility for specific uniformed public services.

You will need to research the government departments responsible for uniformed public services and find out how they manage, monitor and support the specific uniformed public services they are responsible for.

This includes the relationship between central government and inspectorates and other regulators in the process of managing the performance of uniformed public services.

It also covers the complex inter-relationship of central government with devolved governments in the UK, regional assemblies such as the GLA and local councils and statutory bodies such as Police Authorities who may have responsibilities for joint funding and management of uniformed public services.

To achieve P3 you will need to describe how three of those departments undertake their responsibilities for specific uniformed services. Try to select departments to write up for your assignment that have responsibilities for different types of uniformed public services

(ie armed forces, emergency services, other uniformed services).

P4 explain the development process of government policies

M3 analyse the development process of government policies

To achieve these criteria you will need to investigate how government policy is first considered and how it is then turned into law.

You will need to think about the development and consultation process used by government to ensure proposed legislation is supported by the public (individuals, interested pressure groups, businesses).

You will also need to understand the legal processes in parliament that Bills progress through until they are signed by the monarch and become Acts or statutes.

The difference between work that achieves P4 and that which achieves M3 is not so much about quantity, but quality.

Explaining processes is quite straightforward – a description of what happens, how, why and when. To analyse you will need to study or examine in detail, in order to discover more about essential features and how they are related.

41

ACTIVITY 1 (P3)

UK CENTRAL GOVERNMENT DEPARTMENTS AND GOVERNMENT MINISTERS

Use the websites listed below to research the following government departments and their responsibilities for different uniformed public services.

1) Find out who currently holds each of these government posts and their key functions:
 - Prime Minister
 - Deputy Prime Minister
 - Chancellor of the Exchequer
 - Home Secretary
 - Foreign Secretary
 - Speaker of the House of Commons.

2) Find out who holds these key civil service posts and their accountabilities:
 - Cabinet Secretary and Head of the Home Civil Service
 - Permanent Secretary of the Treasury
 - Director General of the Prison Service.

3) Focusing on the departments listed below, which have key responsibilities for UK uniformed public services, find out who is the current Minister of State in overall charge of each department and which Minister in the department is specifically responsible for the uniformed public service(s) that that government department oversees (eg, as you can see in Case Study 1, the Armed Forces themselves come under the responsibility of the Minister of State for Armed Forces, and the MoD Police and the Cadet under the responsibilities of the Minister for Veterans who is a Parliamentary Under-Secretary of State).

- Home Office
- Ministry of Justice
- Department of Transport
- Department of Health
- HM Revenue and Customs
- Department of Communities and Local Government
- Ministry of Defence.

These websites should help with your research:

www.direct.gov.uk
www.civilservice.gov.uk
http://police.homeoffice.gov.uk
www.dh.gov.uk
www.communities.gov.uk
www.hmrc.gov.uk
www.dft.gov.uk
www.mod.uk
www.cabinetoffice.gov.uk/ministerial_responsibilities/downloads/lmr.pdf

ACTIVITY 2 (P3)

1) Using Case study 1 review the various responsibilities of the MOD Ministers.

How is the MoD (and its Ministers) held accountable to both the Cabinet and to Parliament?

How does the MoD interface with the various Heads of the Armed Forces?

2) As a whole class discuss the quotation below which was taken from a lecture by General Sir Mike Jackson, who recently retired as head of the British Army. What are the key points being made about the role of the MoD and its relationship with the Armed Forces?

The MoD, the Ministry of Defence, is very much part of the equation. The role of the MoD is to translate the Government's political objectives into military capabilities and military operations; it's therefore both a Department of State and the supreme headquarters of the Armed Forces. These two roles can be uneasy bedfellows, and that unease can be to the detriment of the Armed Forces.

www.bbc.co.uk 7 December 2006

Case study 1 – Responsibilities of the MOD

The Ministry of Defence (MoD) provides the defence capabilities to ensure the security and defence of the United Kingdom and the Overseas Territories. It supports the government's foreign policy objectives, particularly those relating to peace and security.

The MoD has responsibility for the Armed Forces, including 200,000 regular members of Army, Royal Navy and Royal Air Force, together with over 47,000 reserves.

It is the lead department in the government's policy of defence diplomacy through the North Atlantic Treaty Organisation (NATO), Western European Union and the United Nations. It provides strategic direction on UK participation in conflict prevention, crisis management and operations.

The MoD procures equipment through the Defence Procurement Agency which most cost effectively meets agreed military requirements, including fighter aircraft, tanks and submarines. It also supports British defence exports, within the framework of the government's arms sales policy.

The MoD funds the Meteorological Office, which provides the national weather forecasting service. It also operates military schools and academies, including the Royal Military Academy at Sandhurst. The MoD provides services for military veterans, including war pensions, through the Veterans Agency.

Source: www.pm.gov.uk

Secretary of State for Defence: Responsibilities

Policy including nuclear issues and European defence
Operations, personnel, finance and efficiency
Oversight of major acquisition decisions and defence industrial issues
Media and communications

Minister of State (Armed Forces): Responsibilities

Defence policy and planning, including: arms control and disarmament; export licensing; international organisations; US visiting forces; size and shape of the Armed Forces; intelligence and security, including counter terrorism

Operations, including: overseas commitments and garrisons; Northern Ireland; military aid to the civil authorities; nuclear accident response; military assistance overseas

The Armed Forces (regular and reserves), including: readiness; sustainability; equipment support; performance; collective training; reputation

Defence logistics organisation and logistics transformation

Regional issues and the devolved administrations

Parliamentary Under-Secretary of State (Minister for Veterans): Responsibilities

Veterans affairs, including: legal veterans' health issues; POWs; War Graves; medals and memorials; commemorative events

43

Defence estates, including: defence estates acquisitions and disposals; Service housing; heritage and historic buildings

Services personnel issues, including: recruitment, basic training and education; pay and compensation; equal opportunities; defence medical services; cadets; claims casework; Service families, and Service children's education; Armed Forces Bill

Other issues, including: civilian personnel policy and casework; MoD Police; health and safety; Hydrographic Office and Met Office; non-departmental public bodies; low flying; visits by peers and MPs/Armed Forces Parliamentary Scheme

Minister of State (Minister for Defence Procurement): Responsibilities

Acquisition policy, including: policy; the Forward Equipment Programme; equipment and logistics support project approvals; equipment disposals; nuclear procurement and disposal (including the Atomic Weapons Establishment); Defence Procurement Agency; Defence Logistics Organisation acquisition; defence industrial issues; international collaboration

Defence science and technology, including: policy; international collaboration; Defence Science and Technology Laboratories

Defence exports, including: policy; Defence Export Services Organisation; marketing campaigns; defence issues in the House of Lords

www.cabinetoffice.gov.uk/ministerial_responsibilities/departments/mod.asp

ACTIVITY 3 (P3)

The police forces in England and Wales are managed locally by their Police Authority, but the overall strategy and values for the Police Services are set by the government via the Home Secretary. The police are funded through a local 'precept' from Council Tax payers and local businesses and from direct central government grant.

The budget for 2007/8 for the West Midlands Police was £595.2 million, 70 per cent of which came from central government funds.

The police forces are managed on a day-to-day basis by a Chief Constable and their Police Authority and are accountable to the general public, their local community (who help fund them) and the government and parliament via the Home Office.

They are required to produce performance reports which are public documents and show how well they are achieving against the targets set both nationally and locally.

The police are also subject to inspection by HM Inspectorate of Constabulary (HMIC), subject to audit (by the Audit Commission) and required to cooperate with investigations by the Independent Police Complaints Commission (IPCC) and act on any findings.

a) Find out how your local police force is funded.

b) Find out how it is doing in terms of performance measures.

c) How did the latest HMIC inspection rate your local force?

d) Have there been any recent complaints investigated? What were the outcomes?

e) What do you think are the Home Office powers and responsibilities in relation to the Police Authorities, the Chief Constables, HMIC, IPCC?

These websites will help with your research:

http://noms.homeoffice.gov.uk   www.ind.homeoffice.gov.uk

http://inspectorates.homeoffice.gov.uk   www.ipcc.gov.uk.

ACTIVITY 4 (P3)

Using the information provided in Case study 2 as your starting point, hold a class discussion on the probable reasons for the government restructuring the Home Office and establishing the Ministry of Justice.

Why does the article refer to 'Whitehall'?

How logical do you think the new accountabilities of each department are?

There has been some criticism of the fact that the new Ministry of Justice includes both the courts and those organisations upholding the orders of the courts (NOMS – Prisons and Probation). Do you think this is justified?

Case study 2

Tony Blair gave the go-ahead today for the Home Office to split in two and hand over many of its responsibilities to the Department for Constitutional Affairs. The change, which will not require parliamentary approval, will take effect on 9 May 2007 and is the largest Whitehall shake-up since Labour came to power in 1997. The reshaping will give the Home Office overall control over Britain's battle against crime and terrorism. As well as his control of the police and MI5, Mr Reid will have day-to-day access to the Secret Intelligence Service (MI6) and the eavesdropping agency, GCHQ, although both will remain formally under the oversight of the Foreign Office.

The Home Office will retain its responsibilities for border control and immigration policy but prisons, the probation service and sentencing policy will handed to a new Ministry of Justice: the renamed Department for Constitutional Affairs. The Lord Chancellor will become the Secretary of State for Justice and take charge of the Government's new National Offender Management System (NOMS) which is intended to join up the handling of offenders from the moment they are convicted, through probation to their eventual release and reintegration back into society.

The Home Office was founded in March 1782 as the Home Department. Well known Secretaries of State for the Home

Department include Robert Peel, founder of the police service; Lord Palmerston; Winston Churchill; Roy Jenkins; James Callaghan.

Recent Home Office Problems:

- 1999 Approximately 500 000 people wait up to 50 days after failure of new computer system at Passport Agency

- 2002 Backlog of applications after poor launch of £940 million Criminal Records Bureau

- 2004–05 Home Office loses control of its finances. National Audit Office refuses to give seal of approval

- 2006 Total of 1 025 foreign prisoners released without being considered for deportation

- 2006 The Prison Service runs out of places in jails

- 2007 Disclosure of 27 500 backlog of files on British citizens convicted abroad

- 2007 Runs out of prison places again

The new look Home Office: Overseeing the police, MI5, and borders. There will be an Immigration and Nationality Directorate with 15 944 employees and an Identity Cards and Passport Service with 2 886 staff.

The new Ministry of Justice: (the new Department of Constitutional Affairs)

In charge of probation, criminal justice policy, sentencing, drugs and crime reduction. A staff of 47 100 for prisons and 1 256 for the National Offender Management Service.

Source: www.timesonline.co.uk/tol/news/politics/article1585413.ece

46

Case study 3 – The Greater London Authority

City Hall is home to the Mayor of London, the London Assembly and the GLA, who in July 2002 became tenants of this striking rounded glass building on the south bank of the Thames near Tower Bridge. Members of the public may visit parts of City Hall Monday to Friday from 8 am to 8 pm and on occasional weekends.

The Greater London Authority's main areas of responsibility are: transport; policing; fire and emergency planning; economic development; planning; culture; environment; health.

How is the GLA structured? There is a clear separation of powers within the GLA between the Mayor – who has an executive role, making decisions on behalf of the GLA – and the Assembly, which has a scrutiny role and is responsible for appointing GLA staff. The internal organisation of the GLA takes account of this separation.

The GLA has a pool of permanent staff who support the work of the Mayor and the London Assembly. The Chief Executive oversees the permanent staff of the GLA and ensures that it operates effectively and properly. The Mayor has an office of around 30 staff who support him in his role and direct staff on his behalf. The GLA has taken over control of a number of existing government programmes in London on police, fire, transport and economic development and regeneration. The total budget amounted to £4.7 billion in 2002/03.

The existing London Fire and Civil Defence Authority was reconstituted on 3 July 2000 as the London Fire and Emergency Planning Authority (LFEPA), which is directly accountable to the Mayor. There are 17 members of the LFEPA, nine from the London Assembly and eight nominated by the London boroughs.

For fire, the LFEPA: sets the strategy for the provision of fire services; ensures the fire brigade can meet all normal requirements efficiently; ensures members of the fire brigade are properly trained and equipped; ensures effective arrangements are in place to receive fire calls and deal with them promptly; ensures information likely to be useful for firefighting is gathered; ensures arrangements for advice and guidance on fire prevention are made.

For emergency planning, the LFEPA holds and fulfils the following responsibilities by law: assists the London boroughs with all aspects of planning for emergencies on request; the preparation, review, revision and testing of off-site emergency plans for industrial sites; the preparation and updating of arrangements for the distribution of information to the public in the event of a radiological incident in London; the preparation and updating of emergency plans for 350 kilometres of pipelines that fall within the Pipeline Safety Regulations within London.

The Mayor appoints the members of the LFEPA and its Chair and sets the LFEPA's budget. The Assembly examines and approves the Mayor's budget for the fire and emergency planning services, keeps a close watch on the overall performance of the LFEPA and provides nine members to sit on the LFEPA's board.

ACTIVITY 5 (P3)

Using Case Study 3 as a starting point, review the specific responsibilities that the Mayor of London and the GLA have for uniformed public services in London.

What advantages do you think this coordinated approach has in the Greater London area?

The London Fire and Emergency Planning Authority has wider responsibilities than most Fire and Rescue Services have elsewhere in England and Wales.

- What are they?
- Why do you think it was considered necessary to give the LFEPA these additional powers?
- Do you think this will help in the event of terrorist threats and attacks on London?

Case study 4 – A tale of two Ambulance Services

Over 2000 emergency and urgent staff respond to over 280,000 emergency and urgent incidents every year. To offer an even more flexible responce, the total frontline fleet strength of the South Central Ambulance Services NHS Trust (SCAS) incorporates:

- 100 rapid response vehicles
- 6 rapid response motorbikes
- 182 frontline vehicles
- 95 operational support vehicles

They have assistance from 197 patient transport service vehicles, over 1000 community responders, as well as support from 35 BASICS doctors across the counties and two air ambulance services (the Hampshire & Isle of Wight Air Ambulance and the Thames Valley & Chiltern Air Ambulance)

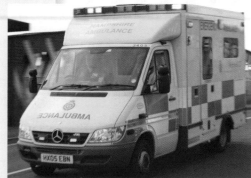

South Central Ambulance Service Performance – April 2006 – March 2007			
Category	Category A:	Category B:	Category C:
	A life threatening incident (LTI)	A serious but not life threatening incident	Other emergencies that are not immediately life threatening or serious
South Central Ambulance response	8 min response: 73.64% 19 min response: 94.92%	19 min response: 91.26%	The service is not currently assessed against this measure
Government Requirement	75% within 8 min 95% within 19 min	95% within 19 minutes	Should receive the most appropriate response

South Central Ambulance Service NHS Trust is investing almost £20 million over the next 18 months in improvements to patient services and staffing levels.

A report from the Audit Commission found that in less than 15 months between April 2005 and July 2006 staff in Wiltshire Ambulance Service altered the timing of 594 emergency calls to make it appear that ambulances had reached callers within the target of eight minutes. Staff also altered the details of 89 lower-priority calls, which are supposed to be reached in 19 minutes. Many changes were made to call categories to make results look better.

Despite these changes, Wiltshire Ambulance Service (now amalgamated into Great Western Ambulance Service) failed to meet the targets for either the 'immediately life threatening' category A calls or the 'serious' category B calls. Richard Lott, the auditor, said: 'The key performance indicator for ambulance trusts is how quickly the ambulance arrives. It is crucially important that the public has confidence in the integrity of the data.'

Last August the Department of Health admitted widespread altering of ambulance figures. A report showed that six out of 31 trusts had misreported response times. Wiltshire was not among them.

Source: The Times, 31 March 2007

ACTIVITY 6 (P3)

Using Case study 4 and research into your own local NHS Ambulance Trust:

a) Evaluate the performance standards set for ambulance services in general and the performance of your own ambulance service

b) Do you think the targets set encourage better performance, or do they encourage errors in reporting?

c) The article from *The Times* mentions there being 31 NHS Ambulance Trusts in August 2006. By April 2007 mergers had seen that number reduced to 13.

Why do you think the government is encouraging regionalisation of the emergency services? What advantages and disadvantages might arise from the creation of large regional emergency services? (For example, will better air ambulance and paramedic services be available?)

(This will be considered in more detail when you produce your assignment work for P6, M4, D2 for Unit 1)

d) Detail the central government department and the various Inspectorates responsible for overseeing the performance of the ambulance services.

NHS Ambulance Trusts at April 2007:

1 East Midlands Ambulance Service NHS Trust
2 East Of England Ambulance Service NHS Trust
3 Great Western Ambulance Service NHS Trust
4 Isle Of Wight NHS PCT
5 London Ambulance Service NHS Trust
6 North East Ambulance Service NHS Trust
7 North West Ambulance Service NHS Trust
8 South Central Ambulance Service NHS Trust
9 South East Coast Ambulance Service NHS Trust
10 South Western Ambulance Service NHS Trust
11 Staffordshire Ambulance Service NHS Trust
12 West Midlands Ambulance Service NHS Trust
13 Yorkshire Ambulance Service NHS Trust

Contact details and geographic coverage can be found at:

www.nhs.uk/England/AuthoritiesTrusts/Ambulance/list.aspx

ACTIVITY 7 (P4, M3)

THE DEVELOPMENT OF GOVERNMENT POLICY – THE INSPIRATION

The idea, or inspiration, for a piece of legislation can come from a variety of sources, including political parties (often as part of their election manifesto) and government departments, interest groups and research organisations, consumer or trade associations, or expert bodies. Sometimes a piece of legislation is introduced in order to make an international treaty or a Directive from the European Union part of United Kingdom law.

Government departments also think ahead, by commissioning research, seeing how other countries tackle similar problems, and holding discussions with relevant European Union bodies and international organisations.

The Cabinet decides what the priorities are for each legislative session. A session lasts about a year, usually starting around November. The Parliamentary timetable has room for only a limited number of major Bills in each session, generally about 15–20.

The Cabinet has to balance manifesto commitments, the demands of individual government departments and other priorities. Once the decision has been taken to go ahead with a particular proposal, the next step of writing the Bill can begin.

Source: www.pm.gov.uk

a) In groups, select one of the main political parties to research. Find out what policies were in their most recent election manifesto.

b) Find out what recent UK legislation has come about as a result of an EU Directive and whether it passed through parliament without opposition.

ACTIVITY 8 (P4, M3)

THE DEVELOPMENT OF GOVERNMENT POLICY – CONSULTATION PROCESSES

White Papers are issued by the government. They set out policy. Although there may be a consultation on the detail of the proposed legislation the intent to turn policy into law is clear.

Green Papers are more open – often known as consultation documents – and usually propose a strategy or actions and invite public views and feedback.

In January 2004 the Cabinet Office published a Code of Practice on Consultation which can be downloaded from the site below. It lays down 6 principles which should be followed for all proposed legislation. These are listed below:

1) Consult widely throughout the process, allowing a minimum of 12 weeks for written consultation at least once during the development of the policy.

2) Be clear about what your proposals are, who may be affected, what questions are being asked and the timescale for responses.

3) Ensure that your consultation is clear, concise and widely accessible.

4) Give feedback regarding the responses received and how the consultation process influenced the policy.

5) Monitor your department's effectiveness at consultation, including the use of a designated consultation coordinator.

6) Ensure your consultation follows better regulation best practice, including carrying out a Regulatory Impact Assessment if appropriate.

Source: www.cabinetoffice.gov.uk/regulation/documents/consultation/pdf/code.pdf

Current consultations are listed at government department websites such as www.dca.gov.uk/consult/confr.htm

Work in groups to find out:

1) How political party policy gets translated into White and Green Papers.

2) What the concept of 'Cabinet joint responsibility' means.

3) Examples of proposed legislation that were modified or discontinued because of public opposition during the consultation process.

ACTIVITY 9 (P4, M3)

THE DEVELOPMENT OF GOVERNMENT POLICY – LOBBYING PARLIAMENT

Lobbying is the practice of individuals and organisations trying to influence the opinions of MPs and members of the House of Lords. Methods of lobbying vary and can include sending letters, making presentations, providing briefing material to Members and organised rallies.

Anyone can lobby an MP or member of the House of Lords. Examples are:

- Individual members of the public
- Groups of constituents
- Local businesses
- Organised pressure groups/campaigners
- Commercial organisations.

MPs and members of the Huse of Lords are the target of many different lobbying interests. Often the result these lobbyists are seeking is for the MP or member of the House of Lords to vote a certain way on a specific issue. However, this decision will ultimately be down to the MP or Lord's own judgement and the influence (if any) that existing party policy will have on them.

Source: www.parliament.uk/about/contacting/lobbying.cfm

1) In groups, identify a pressure group to investigate. (Some well known ones are listed below, but most charities also act as pressure groups for specific issues, as do political parties and many special-interest groups.)

2) Find out what parliamentary lobbying campaigns they have been involved in. How successful have they been in initiating change in legislation or modifying planned legislation?

www.greenpeace.org.uk	Greenpeace UK
www.cfoi.org.uk	Campaign for Freedom Of Information
www.liberty-human-rights.org.uk	Liberty
www.electoral-reform.org.uk	The Electoral Reform Society
www.cnduk.org	Campaign for Nuclear Disarmament
www.ash.org.uk	Action on Smoking & Health UK
www.foe.co.uk	Friends of the Earth

Other well known pressure groups can be located at:

www.uknetguide.co.uk/News_and_Weather/Organisations/Pressure_Groups.html

ACTIVITY 10 (P4, M3)

THE LEGAL PROCESS OF CREATING LEGISLATION IN THE UK

The procedure for passing the different types of Bills is broadly similar in both Houses. At a very simple level, a Bill must pass through several stages – in both Houses – to become a law.

The following stages take place in both Houses:

- First reading (formal introduction of the Bill without debate)
- Second reading (general debate)
- Committee stage (detailed examination, debate and amendments. In the House of Commons this stage takes place in a Public Bill Committee)
- Report stage (opportunity for further amendments)
- Third reading (final chance for debate – amendments are possible in the Lords).

When a Bill has passed through both Houses it is returned to the first House (where it started) for the second House's amendments to be considered.

Both Houses must agree on the final text. There may be several rounds of exchanges between the two Houses until agreement is reached on every word of the Bill. Once this happens the Bill proceeds to the next stage: Royal Assent – the Bill is signed by the monarch.

It is now an Act of Parliament (the proposals of the Bill have now become law).

www.parliament.uk/about/how/laws/stages.cfm explains the process in detail!

1) Research a Bill that is currently before parliament.

2) Find out if it is a Government Bill or a Private Members Bill – what is the difference? Was it announced in the Queen's Speech? Does this matter?

3) Does the Bill have cross-party support? What does this mean?

4) Find an example of a Government Bill that has been delayed or blocked by the House of Lords.

5) What is a 'guillotine' in terms of getting Bills though parliament? Why is it used?

6) What is Royal Assent? What would happen if the monarch refused to sign legislation passed by parliament?

www.commonsleader.gov.uk/output/Page1745.asp will give you a list of current government bills.

www.parliament.uk/about/how/laws.cfm

www.parliament.uk/factsheets have some useful further information.

ACTIVITY 11 (P4, M3)

Case study 5 details the process of a controversial idea becoming legislation and then the issues with implementing the relevant Act.

In this example the Gambling Act 2005 has received Royal Assent but the implementation has been blocked in the House of Lords.

1) As a whole class discuss the following issues:

a) Why was the legislation controversial? Do you agree with the concerns raised by those opposing this legislation?

b) Do you think the House of Lords should have the power to block a measure approved in the elected House of Commons?

2) Individually research the implementation process for a specific Act of Parliament.

Case study 5 – The timetable of introducing super casinos in the UK

- Before 1960: all casinos illegal in the UK.
- 1960 Gaming Act allowed casinos.
- 1968 Gaming Act introduced regulation and all 130 plus UK casinos come under the regulation of the Gaming Board.
- 26 March 2002: Labour unveils plans to shake up gambling laws paving the way for Britain first Las Vegas-style super-casinos.
- 19 October 2004: Government publishes the Gambling Bill to sweep away limits on the number of slot machines and cash prizes, and membership restrictions.
- 1 Nov 2004: Tessa Jowell forced to promise a cap on the number of casinos to get the Bill through.
- The Gambling Commission was set up under the Gambling Act 2005.

- 5 April 2005: Government concedes there will be only one regional super casino instead of eight previously planned.

- The Gambling Act 2005 received Royal Assent in April 2005. It was expected to come fully info force by Autumn 2007.

- 24 May 2006: shortlist of possible sites for first super-casino announced. Wembley Stadium (which later dropped out) and Millennium Dome, Cardiff, Blackpool, Manchester, Newcastle, Sheffield and Glasgow are on the list.

- 2 September 2006: a super-casino would be a social disaster, acting as a magnet for Mafia gangs, drug dealers and prostitutes, according to a report by the council which wanted a gambling complex at Wembley.

- 15 January 2007: reports by police and health experts warn that super-casinos will cause a crime wave and an epidemic of problem gambling, especially among children.

- 30 January 2007: Manchester chosen as location for the super-casino, beating Blackpool and the Dome, which were bookmakers' favourites.

- 21 March 2007: Chancellor Gordon Brown announces a 50 per cent tax on casino profits – a huge disincentive to gambling operators.

- March 2007: Commons vote for the order by 274 to 250.

- 28 March 2007: The House of Lords voted against the government order on casinos so rejecting the plans for the super-casino in Manchester. Peers voted 123 votes to 120 for an amendment sending the government's entire casino package back to the planning stage.

- As she is unable to bring the same order to the Commons for six months, it is possible Ms Jowell could split the package, asking the Lords to approve the less controversial smaller casinos first.

Key source: www.mailonsunday.co.uk/pages/live/articles/news/news.html?in_article_id=445269&in_page_id=1770

In this section we are focusing on P4, P5, P6, M3, D2 from Unit 2 – 'Team Leadership in the Uniformed Public Services'. (This unit also links to Unit 4 – Team Development in Public Services.)

These grading criteria cover the theoretical understanding of the types of teams that might exist in specific uniformed public services and different theories and models of the stages of team development.

You will also look at the qualities and skills needed to lead a team effectively and potential barriers to effective team performance that have to be successfully managed by the team leader in order to plan and achieve specific tasks. (P5, P6)

You will then get the chance to apply these theoretical concepts in a number of practical contexts. *If your class is also going to study Unit 4 'Team Development in Uniformed Public Services' (which is a Core Unit for both National Certificate and National Diploma) then the activities in this section will also provide evidence towards P6, M3, D2 from that Unit, where you have to take part in five team activities, evaluate your performance and recommend personal development for future teamwork activities.*

You will be given opportunities to demonstrate practical examples of effective leadership of the team in planning and undertaking specific tasks. (P4, M3)

You will then need to evaluate how effectively you led the team and plan your development so that your leadership effectiveness is improved. (D2)

Content

4) Understand what makes an effective team

Developing the team: types of team, eg work teams, project teams, cross-functional teams, inter-service teams; stages in team development eg forming, norming, storming, performing, transforming

Barriers to effective performance: lack of commitment, eg leader, team member; poor communication; lack of appropriate skills; resource issues eg financial, physical, staff; personal factors, eg challenges to authority, conflict between team members

Evaluation methods: goals achieved; assessment of own team's performance; identification of skills gap; recommendations for future; reflect on own practice.

3) Be able to use appropriate skills and qualities to lead a team

Skills and qualities: eg time management, commitment, motivational, delegation skills

Implementing a plan: identify primary aim(s); consider factors, eg available resources, team member capabilities; select course of action

Leading the team: brief team; check understanding including overall aim, individual roles; execute plan; ongoing quality control, eg of safety, of performance; achieve aim; debrief team; review and evaluation.

Grading criteria

P6 describe different types of teams and the stages of team development.

You will need to understand and be able describe the types of teams which exist in the various uniformed public services including teams made up of personnel from a number of different public services working together. You will need to understand the stages that teams may go through from being first set up to maximising their performance and then disbanding once the task or project is completed.

P5 describe evaluation methods used to assess effective team leadership

You will need to understand how leaders ensure their teams perform effectively and how the effectiveness of both the leader and the team can be measured and potential barriers to effective performance removed.

P4 use appropriate skills to lead a team in the practical implementation of a plan

M3 demonstrate effective leadership skills when leading a team in the practical implementation of a plan to achieve a given task

D2 evaluate own ability to provide effective team leadership, making recommendations for own development and improvement

To achieve these grading criteria you will need to lead a team in a number of situations and demonstrate appropriate skills in that role so that the team can plan and achieve given tasks. You will then need to evaluate your leadership skills, highlighting strengths and limitations and draw up an action plan to improve and develop the effectiveness of your leadership skills.

Because these are practical criteria you will need to take advantage of all the opportunities you get to lead teams (both across the whole of your BTEC programme and also in other contexts eg as captain of a sports team or leading an activity in the Cadets) and log those opportunities, ideally undertaking some analysis of what skills you demonstrated, how well the team did in planning and undertaking tasks and whether the goals were achieved. There are sample logs and evaluation tools included in this student guide which you could use or adapt for logging you own performance as team leader.

Wherever possible your log should be authenticated by your tutor or instructor and also by members of the teams you have led. If you are leading practical activities then think about taking photos to record your achievements and add to your log. It is also useful for the team to evaluate their performance both as a team and individually. Using an objective observer for some tasks will give another perspective of team and leadership effectiveness.

ACTIVITY 1 (P6)

TYPES OF TEAMS IN THE UNIFORMED PUBLIC SERVICES

The table overleaf provides a useful starting point for understanding the types of teams found in the uniformed public services. Identify one specific uniformed public service and see how many of those teams might exist. When would they be used and why?

You might find this information on relevant websites and in news articles, but it would be really valuable to talk to a member of your chosen uniformed public service and find out their experiences of different types of team working.

Once you have investigated your chosen service, share your findings with other students in the group (you could make a poster, give a short briefing, make a presentation).

My chosen uniformed service			
Type of team	**Purpose**	**Examples of when used**	**Examples of why used**
Work teams			
Project teams			
Cross-functional teams			
Inter-service teams			
Other types of teams in my chosen service			

ACTIVITY 2 (P6)

MODELS OF TEAM DEVELOPMENT

Bruce Tuckman's model

Groups go through various stages as they develop to effective team working. A common model used to track the development of groups was suggested by B.W. Tuckman and outlines five stages of team development. These are:

Forming – Characterised by polite and well mannered greeting. Members also check-out their feelings regarding membership of the group, what roles they may take and what the purpose of the group is.

Storming – Typically this can be an uncomfortable time for groups where members are often testing the limits and exploring what is possible. Rebelliousness, competition and the setting up of cliques are all features of this stage.

Norming – At this stage the group is beginning to work through its conflicts and agree on ways of functioning towards effective performance.

Performing – Now the team is working together towards a common goal.

All teams will develop at different speeds and some may get stuck in one of the phases. The important thing is to be aware of the subtle and intricate dynamics of the group development process.

Mourning or transforming – The team comes to the end of its life and moves on, either to disband or to reform in a new structure or with new membership.

a) Find out more details of these team development stages – one useful site is: www.businessballs.com/tuckmanformingstormingnormingperforming.htm

b) Use this model to analyse your team after you have completed a range of team activities.

57

ACTIVITY 3 (P6)

PETER HONEY'S VIEWS ON TEAMS

Honey identified three stages that teams might progress through.

Stage 1 – The chaotic stage – People are thrown together and given a task to tackle and often both the leader and team members underestimate the complexities of getting a team to work effectively.

Stage 2 – The formal stage – After experiencing chaos the team will recognise the need for structure, rules and defined roles, including the leadership role. Objectives and goals will be defined as will the processes to achieve these.

Stage 3 – The skilful stage – At this point the team learn to work effectively together, and procedures and tight role boundaries can be relaxed. The team understands individual strengths and weaknesses and trusts each other. Leadership can be less directive and more consultative.

MICHAEL WOODCOCK'S THEORY OF TEAM DEVELOPMENT

The Undeveloped Team – Feelings are avoided, objectives are uncertain; the leader makes decisions. Once group members have spent time together, they will develop.

The Experimenting Team – Issues are faced more openly, listening takes place, the team may become temporarily introspective. More listening may happen because team members have overcome problems; the issues that are talked about in the group will be easier to deal with.

The Consolidating Team – Personal interaction is established on a cooperative basis, the task is clarified, objectives agreed and tentative procedures implemented. A sign of the team changing and getting better is that members talk about the tasks in a non-threatening manner, making it easier for people to speak, so everyone is able to understand the task. At this stage there are unlikely to be passengers within the group.

The Mature Team – Feelings are open, a wide range of options considered, working methods are methodical, leadership style is contributory, individuals are flexible and the group recognises its responsibility to the rest of the organisation. Team members try to include different ideas in the task. They also like to make sure the work is clear and in order, so it is precise with no flaws in it. Everyone makes a contribution and the leadership may be taken by different individuals as appropriate to the current task.

a) As a whole class, discuss the two models of team development shown above. What similarities and differences are there?

b) Use these models to help you when you are leading team activities later in this guide.

ACTIVITY 4

ANALYSING MY OWN EFFECTIVENESS (UNIT 2 D2; UNIT 4 D2)

SWOT Analysis is a very effective analytical tool. It can be used on a personal basis as suggested here. It can also be used on a team basis after you have worked on a number of projects and tasks together. It is used by organisations to analyse organisational effectiveness. On a personal level you can use it to analyse both your leadership effectiveness and your team worker performance.

Strengths

- What advantages do you have?
- What do you do well?
- What relevant resources (eg people, time, materials, experience etc) do you have access to?
- What do other people see as your strengths?

Consider this from your own point of view and from the point of view of the people you deal with. Don't be modest. Be realistic. If you are having any difficulty with this, try writing down a list of your characteristics. Some of these will hopefully be strengths!

Weaknesses

- What could you improve?
- What developmental feedback have you received in the past?
- What should you avoid?

Again, you are considering this from an internal and external basis: do other people seem to perceive weaknesses that you do not see?

Opportunities

- What are the opportunities facing you?
- What are the immediate challenges you are aware of?

Useful opportunities can come from such things as the work you do on your BTEC National programme (both classroom based and outdoors, or activity based), hobbies and interests, sports, family events.

A useful approach to looking at opportunities is to look at your strengths and ask yourself whether these open up any opportunities. Alternatively, look at your weaknesses and ask yourself whether you could open up opportunities by eliminating them.

Threats

- What obstacles do you face?
- Could any of your weaknesses seriously threaten your success?

Create a SWOT table like the one on the next page, and carry out a personal SWOT analysis.

(Case studies 1 & 2 may provide some ideas as they are based on leadership competences defined by HM Prison Service and the Royal Navy)

Personal SWOT analysis

Strengths	Weaknesses
1	1
2	2
3	3
4	
5	
Opportunities	Threats
1	1
2	2
3	3
4	
5	

How can your weaknesses be addressed and threats turned into opportunities?

How could the use of SWOT analysis help you in leading or developing your team?

ACTIVITY 5

GAP ANALYSIS – EVALUATING DEVELOPMENT NEEDS (UNIT 2 D2; UNIT 4 D2)

Gap analysis is used by a number of uniformed public services as part of their staff development planning process. An example of its use by Hampshire F&R services can be found at www.hantsfire.gov. uk/skills_gap_analysis.

Use the format below to help you define your personal leadership development and improvement plan.

(Case Studies 1 & 2 may provide some ideas as they are based on leadership competences defined by HM Prison Service and the Royal Navy.)

Step One: Define where you want to be – your goal

Describe what it will feel like when you have achieved your goal

Step Two: Clarify where you are

Where are you now? What are your key strengths and identified development needs?

Step Three: Identify enablers and constraints

Enablers (things that will help me achieve my goals) are:

Constraints (things that will get in the way of achieving my goals) are:

Step Four: Prioritise

To strengthen your enablers and diminish the impact of the constraints you need to prioritise – what should you work on first?

Step Five: Plan action

Key Issue 1	Required Action	Who is Involved	Review Date
Key Issue 2	Required Action	Who is Involved	Review Date

Case study 1 – HM Prison Service Core Competences

HM Prison Service has defined 12 competences that staff should display. Amongst these are Team Playing and Networking; Team Building and Liaison; Leadership and Decision Making. When applying for an initial post in HM Prison Service or applying for a specialist post or promotion internally, applicants are expected to explain how they meet the competence requirements of the post applied for. The form in Activity 6B is one format used by HM Prison Service for this purpose. More information, details of all 12 competences and application processes are available at: www.hmprisonservice.gov.uk

Competence 7. Team Playing/Networking

1) Is a good team player who encourages others to contribute.
2) Is capable of interacting easily with a wide range of people, both colleagues and public.
3) Upholds equality of opportunity and actively rejects discrimination.

Performance Indicators

- Is punctual
- Demonstrates support and care for all colleagues
- Shows confidence in others and establishes mutual trust
- Is aware of impact of own behaviour on others
- Acts always to represent the Prison Service well
- Follows instructions, yet uses initiative
- Completes tasks on time wherever possible
- Addresses issues in a positive manner
- Challenges negative behaviour without causing bitterness
- Develops networks to learn from others
- Focuses on team goals and priorities
- Actively upholds equality of opportunity
- Actively rejects any form of discriminatory practice

Competence 8. Team Building/Liaison

1) Is able to get people to work well together.
2) Gains understanding of the need for trust and cooperation to achieve effective working.
3) Can reconcile conflict and build group identity.

Performance Indicators

- Combines individuals' styles and skills to build an effective team
- Identifies strengths and development needs of team(s) and individual(s)
- Guides the work of teams and individuals to achieve organisational objectives
- Monitors and evaluates the performance of teams and individuals

- Shows interest in each team member's achievement
- Acknowledges good work and celebrates success
- Challenges poor work
- Can discipline and reprimand if required
- Fosters atmosphere of honesty, trust and mutual support
- Treats delicate and/or personal issues with sensitivity and discretion
- Consults members before making changes which affect the team
- Briefs teams and individuals on current issues and priorities
- Confronts team difficulties openly and seeks understanding
- Identifies and minimises interpersonal conflict
- Deals with grievances promptly
- Accepts responsibility for action of the team

Competence 12. Leadership and Decision Making

1) Is self assured and decisive, creating a good impression.
2) Inspires confidence.
3) Has vision and knows when to react quickly or take a longer-term view.

Performance Indicators

- Has vision and can communicate it
- Demonstrates self confidence
- Shows humility
- Inspires confidence and loyalty
- Gives praise and recognition where appropriate
- Confronts difficult issues openly
- Is realistic about own strengths and weaknesses
- Actively seeks views
- Accepts challenge but moderates risk
- Represents the organisation both within and outside the Service
- Makes judgements which carry conviction
- Takes decisions within time constraints and delegated authority
- Uses judgement to refer to higher level when appropriate
- Take decisions with restricted information, when necessary
- Amends decisions where appropriate in the light of new information.

63

ACTIVITY 6 (UNIT 2 D2; UNIT 4 D2)

a) As a class discuss these competences – are they a useful guide?

b) Use the performance indicators above as a checklist of your own leadership and teamwork competence. It could be a useful checklist for your SWOT and GAP analysis.

ACTIVITY 7 (UNIT 2 D2; UNIT 4 D2)

As **an effective leader** you will need to be able to explain how you meet the competence requirements of HM Prison Service. For each of the 3 competences listed in the case study (Team Playing and Networking; Team Building and Liaison; Leadership and Decision Making) give an example of where you have demonstrated that competence and analyse that example using the headings in the table below.

What was the situation?
What did you do?
Why did you do it this way?
What was the outcome?
How could you have improved?

Case study 2 – John Adair, leadership development in the Royal Navy

The Royal Navy has always seen itself as an organisation with a wide and diverse range of people. It was the increase in Leadership and Management understanding in the 1950s and 1960s that led to realisation that more than just basic leadership and Naval skills were required. Since the early 1990s a more systematic understanding of the leadership and management skills is required of potential 'leaders'. The three interactive circles of 'Action Centred Leadership' (ACL) theory have become the underlying bedrock, helping to forge a new beginning for the leaders within the Royal Navy within both the Officer and Ratings Corps.

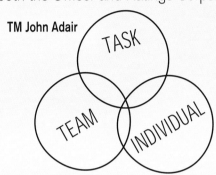

TM John Adair

In order to achieve the task, manage the team or group and manage individuals, the following stages must be considered.

1) Defining the aim:
   a) Identify the task and constraints.
   b) Involve the team.
   c) Share commitments and values.
   d) Clarify individual aims.
   e) SAFETY implications.

2) The Planning – during the planning phase the 'Leader' must:
   a) Utilise the 'SMART' principle: (Specific – Measurable – Achievable – Realistic – Time Bound).
   b) Prioritise – matching resources to the task.
   c) Listen to opinions.
   d) Consider options/contingencies.
   e) Assess the individual's skills/competencies.
   f) Delegate – individual strengths and weaknesses.
   g) Set targets and deadlines.

3) Briefing the plan – as the 'Leader' briefs their plan, they are to:
   a) Be clear and concise.
   b) Offer a concrete solution.
   c) Ensure understanding from team members.
   d) Encourage questions.
   e) Be time conscious.

4) The Execution – while the plan is being executed the 'Leader' will:

   a) Maintain standards.

   b) Effect quality control activities.

   c) Coordinate and control the team's efforts.

   d) Reconcile any conflicts.

5) Evaluation – as the plan is being executed, the 'Leader' will continuously evaluate the situation by:

   a) Maintaining progress.

   b) Reviewing the aim and objectives.

   c) Re-planning and re-briefing as required.
   d) Recognising the success and learning from mistakes.

6) Communication – the 'Leader':
   a) Clarifies the purpose.
   b) May use a map, model or diagram to qualify the requirement.

   c) Will ensure accuracy.

   d) Will act logically.

   e) Will be structured.

   f) Will demonstrate sequential thought.

ACL and the functional, transferable skills, without doubt, work! They are one of the most valued assets in the teaching of Command, Leadership and Management which allows the Royal Navy to train its personnel to understand the concepts of how we do our business, always 'Ready to Fight and Win'. Within the Royal Navy, the title 'Superior Officer' is not awarded lightly; it is a position of responsibility and accountability. This title is afforded to individuals who are looked at by their superiors as people who can adapt to a situation, react in a crisis in adverse conditions and, above all, be decisive in action without hesitation.

Source: www.johnadair.co.uk/articles/royal_navy.pdf

John Adair developed his Action Centred Leadership model while lecturing at Sandhurst Royal Military Academy and has since worked with all the Armed Forces on their leadership development programmes.

a) Research the ways leaders are developed in a range of uniformed public services.

b) Using Adair's ACL model as a starting point, use the practical activities in the rest of this guide as opportunities to apply the following process:

- Define aims
- Plan
- Brief
- Execute
- Evaluate
- Communicate.

ACTIVITY 8

DESIGNING A CHALLENGE FOR THE OTHER TEAMS

In groups of four to six students you are required to plan, prepare, implement and supervise a team activity. You can use your imagination, provided you consider the health and safety issues. You must agree your team challenge with your teacher before carrying it out!

The activity can either take place in the classroom or in the school/college grounds.

Your team will be required to provide any equipment necessary to complete the task.

You will be required to evaluate your performance both as a participant of the activities and as part of the team organising the activity. These are to be submitted after the event.

Some ideas can be found at: www.businessballs.com.

ACTIVITY 9

HOUSE OF CARDS

- Work in small teams of four to six students. Each team has to work together to build a 'house of cards' within 15 minutes, using only the resources listed below.
- This is a competitive event, with each team competing to produce the winning 'house', racing against the other teams to be first to finish successfully.
- All team projects are judged by your teacher (whose ruling is final and cannot be contested).

Project criteria are:
- Efficient use of resources
- Attractiveness
- Height
- Structural integrity
- Presentation

Supplies (resources), one set per team:
- 1 standard pack playing cards
- 1 stack Post-it notes (square)
- 1 box paper clips
- Tape
- Coloured markers

Instructions:
- Each team has 15 minutes to build a house with the resources provided.
- Before getting started the team must select a named leader.

- Your teacher will identify specific criteria for judging successful projects.
- As teams finish, they should chart their finish times on a flipchart.
- Once all teams have finished, walk around with the judge (teacher) to view the work of other teams. (No sabotage is allowed – a disqualification criterion!)
- At their own tables each team should discuss the factors contributing to their success or otherwise.
- Record these factors on a flipchart. The leader will be expected to present their team's findings to the rest of the class.
- The teacher must award a rating for each project (using a scale of 1–5, with 5 being the highest, for each criterion). Highest possible score: 25.

Discussion questions:

- How was team leadership determined – appointed or assumed?
- What unique contributions did each member offer? How did those contributions affect the successful outcome of the project?
- How did the competitive nature of the event affect the quality of the project?
- What have the team learned to improve their performance in future tasks?

Finally:

- Copy and complete the Self Evaluation Sheet below.
- If your tutor has asked someone to take the observer role, they should copy and complete the Observer's Sheet.

Self Evaluation Sheet

Name: ....   Date: ....

Details of team activity:

My role in the team (leader, member, other):

How did I perform?

How did the team perform? Did we achieve the task?

What were my strengths?

What were my weaknesses?

How could I improve my performance?

Student signature: ....   Tutor signature: ....

Observer's Sheet

Copy the form below, then watch the group performing the task and detail your observations on the form.

You must be prepared to give oral feedback and answer group questions on your observations.

Details of the task

Date: .... Group members: ....

Question	Comments
Were people involved and interested?	
Were members of the group getting satisfaction from being in the group?	
Was the atmosphere friendly?	
What happened when there was conflict? Was it dealt with or ignored?	
Did some members participate more than others? Who? Why?	
Who carried out the leadership function? How effective were they?	
Who influenced the most?	
Were there any rivalries? Did the leader handle them?	
How did the leader organise the planning? Did the team stick to the plan?	
Did the leader manage the group and discourage discussion of unrelated matters?	
How did the leader manage the decision-making process? How did this affect the group?	
Were subgroups formed? How did this affect the task?	
How well did the group follow the task instructions?	

Other Comments

Signature of observer: .... Signature of tutor: ....

ACTIVITY 10 (P4, M3, D2)

Work in teams of four to six students. Each team has to complete the task in the brief below.

Brief

Part 1

You are members of the Senior Management Team at Macaroni Production Limited.

You are about to attend a meeting to plan today's production.

You have 30 minutes to choose a leader and come up with a production plan, including costings. This must be agreed by the Quality Control Manager (your tutor) before production can commence.

You are strongly recommended to agree a target. Assess the risks that might affect the activity, and prepare a contingency plan.

Part 2

Your production task for today is to make as many freestanding structures as possible in 50 minutes, using the resources available to purchase. These are spaghetti and marshmallows. As these are being delivered to the site later today you cannot inspect them in advance.

You have a total budget available of £100.

For each structure accepted as suitable you will be paid £5.

Spaghetti costs 50p per stick and marshmallows £1 each.

The quality requirements are that each structure must:
- Be at least 60 cm in height
- Be capable of standing without external support for at least 3 minutes once placed on the Quality Control Manager's desk (tutor)
- The Quality Control Manager has the final say!

Debrief

Part 3

Reconvene your meeting and analyse the outcomes.
- Did you meet your targets?
- Have you made a profit?
- What is your balance?
- Which team is the overall winner?
- Had you identified the potential risks?
- Did you have contingencies? How well did they work out?
- Out of 10, how successful would you rate your team's efforts?
- If you were leader, how effective was your leadership in achieving the plan?
- Alternatively, as a team member, how well did you contribute?

(Keep a record of this as it will be useful as evidence for Unit 4 P6, M3, D2)
- How could you apply this to a real work situation?

ACTIVITY 11

LOST AT SEA (P4, M3, D2)

You are adrift on a yacht in the Pacific Ocean. Much of the yacht and its contents have been destroyed by fire. The yacht is now slowly sinking. You have an inflatable rubber life raft just large enough to carry yourself, the crew and the inventory below. The total contents of the survivors' pockets are a packet of cigarettes, matches and some paper money.

You do not know your exact position because your navigational equipment has been destroyed and because you and your crew were distracted while trying to bring the fire under control. Your best estimate is that you are about 1 000 miles south-south-west of the nearest island.

On the inventory are listed the 15 items left intact and undamaged after the fire. Your task is to put them in order of importance to your crew in helping them to survive. Copy the inventory and place a number 1 by the most important item, a number 2 by the second most important and so on, through to 15, the least important.

Inventory

Sextant ❏   Small transistor radio ❏

Shaving mirror ❏   Shark repellent ❏

Five gallon can of water ❏   Opaque plastic x 20ft ❏

Mosquito netting ❏   One quart of 160 proof rum ❏

One case of rations ❏   Nylon rope x 15ft ❏

Maps of the area ❏   Two boxes of chocolate bars ❏

Seat cushion   Fishing kit ❏
(flotation device) ❏

Two gallon can of oil/petrol
mixture ❏

Complete and score the task, then complete the self and team evaluations!

ACTIVITY 12

HUNDREDS OF BOXES (P4, M3, D2)

The Problem

You are teams of traffic controllers and drivers for a company which specialises in distributing boxes from a company warehouse to shops in neighbouring towns.

Task

Your team is asked to select a leader then:

1) Plan the trips for a single driver delivering boxes to the towns of Acton, Boston, Cardiff and Dover, shown on the Planning Map.

2) Copy and complete the driver's delivery time sheet, then complete your copy showing the time for driving, unloading and on breaks and also the total time at work.

3) Enter each stage of the operation separately on the time sheet.

4) Once the task is completed debrief and evaluate your team performance.

Materials

A planning map

A driver's delivery time-sheet

Coloured pens

A delivery order and the Company Rules (see below)

Time

You have 30 minutes to complete the task.

Assessment

Your team's success will be judged on the economical use of the driver's time.

DELIVERY ORDER

Please Deliver:

500 boxes to our Acton Branch

600 boxes to our Boston Branch

200 boxes to our Cardiff Branch

100 boxes to our Dover Branch

COMPANY RULES

(for planning purposes)

1) A van must not carry more than 1 000 boxes at a time

2) The average speed of a van will not be more than 20 mph

3) Drivers must have a break every 3 hours (taken at the warehouse only)

4) At the warehouse loading is done by two loaders taking 5 minutes for every 100 boxes loaded while the driver takes a break

5) Unloading (by the driver) takes 10 minutes for every 100 boxes delivered

HUNDREDS OF BOXES – Planning map

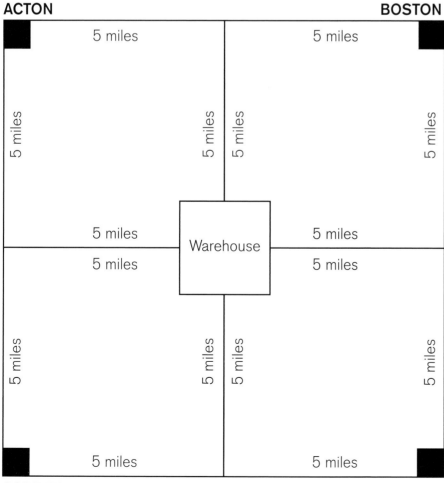

HUNDREDS OF BOXES – Delivery time sheet

1. LOADING		2. DRIVING		3. DELIVERY		2+3 JOURNEY TIME
NO.	TIME	DIST	TIME	NO.	TIME	

TOTAL LOADING TIME ....

\+

TOTAL JOURNEY TIME ....

= TOTAL WORKDAY ....

ACTIVITY 13

BARRIERS TO SUCCESS (P5)

Working in small teams, copy the table below and use it to discuss and evaluate potential barriers to successful team performance.

Potential barrier to achieving team goal	Potential impact	Ways the leader can deal with this
Lack of commitment by the leader		
Lack of team member commitment		
Poor communication		
Lack of appropriate skills to complete the task		
Lack of resources		
■ Financial		
■ Physical		
■ Personnel		
Challenges to the leader's authority		
Conflict in the team		

ACTIVITY 14

MOTIVATING THE TEAM (P4, P5)

McGregor's X/Y theory

Copy the statements below. They represent views which people commonly hold about other people at work. Consider each pair of statements for a few moments and in each case circle the number on the scale which most accurately represents your view.

A People are fundamentally lazy.　　1 2 3 4 5　　People enjoy work and achievement.

B People are only interested in their own benefit.　　1 2 3 4 5　　People have others' interests at heart.

C Punishments get results.　　1 2 3 4 5　　Excessive punishments are counter-productive.

D People have no interest in the work they do.　　1 2 3 4 5　　People are basically interested in their working lives.

E People are basically dishonest.　　1 2 3 4 5　　People are basically honest.

F People are basically sly.　　1 2 3 4 5　　People are basically open in their dealings with others.

G Discipline and control bring the best results.　　1 2 3 4 5　　People respond best when given freedom of action.

H People are not interested in the performance of their team.　　1 2 3 4 5　　People are interested in the performance of their team.

I People dislike responsibility.　　1 2 3 4 5　　People enjoy responsibility.

ANSWERS

ACTIVITY 11

Solution to 'lost at sea'

This exercise was originally used by the US Navy Coastguard in training recruits.

Their view of the correct answer is based on setting the following priorities:

1) Rescue – almost all successful rescues at sea occur within the first 36 hours of the disaster. During this period food and water are less important than signalling devices. If you cannot attract attention you have almost no chance of survival.

2) Survival – next in importance are items to sustain life until rescue arrives.

3) Navigation/movement – articles for navigation/sailing etc are valueless – you cannot reach land. It is too far away. It does not matter where you are, but where your rescuers are!

Against this criteria, the articles available can be prioritised as follows:

1) Shaving mirror – vital for signalling
2) Two gallon can of oil/petrol mixture – vital for signalling – will burn on water
3) Five gallon can of water – top priority for sustaining life
4) One case of rations – life-sustaining in longer term
5) Opaque plastic x 20 ft – to collect rainwater and provide shelter
6) Two boxes of chocolate bars – reserve food supply
7) Fishing kit – ranked lower than rations because there is no guarantee you will catch anything
8) Nylon rope x 15 ft – for securing equipment or constructing sea anchor
9) Seat cushion (floatation device) – life saver if man overboard
10) Shark repellent – obvious
11) One quart of 160 proof rum – valuable as antiseptic but dehydrating if consumed
12) Small transistor radio – useless as it will not transmit
13) Maps of the area – irrelevant
14) Mosquito netting – there are no mosquitoes in the Pacific Ocean
15) Sextant – useless without chronometer and tables.

Scoring system

The objective is to get as close to the 'right' answer as possible. When the inventory has been completed, each item on the inventory will have been given a priority number between 1 and 15. You then need to score the priority accorded to each item. To do this, you need a copy of the solution in front of you. Then for each of the items, calculate the difference between the position in the solution and the position given by your team.

Eg Sextant		
	Position accorded in solution	15
	Position accorded by your team	10
	Score	**5**
Fishing kit	Position accorded in solution	7
	Position accorded by your team	8
	Score	**1**

When you have scored each item on the inventory, you should add up all the scores. This number is the final total. The team with the LOWEST score wins!

ACTIVITY 14

Score sheet

Create a score sheet like the one below, and score each set of statements according to which of the five ratings on each scale you have circled. Do this as follows:

A   1   2   3   4   5

_____   Score   …………..

B   1   2   3   4   5

_____   Score   …………..

C   1   2   3   4   5

_____   Score   …………..

D   1   2   3   4   5

_____   Score   …………..

E   1   2   3   4   5

_____   Score   …………..

F   1   2   3   4   5

_____   Score   …………..

G   1   2   3   4   5

_____   Score   …………..

H   1   2   3   4   5

_____   Score   …………..

I   1   2   3   4   5

_____   Score   …………..

TOTAL SCORE   …………..

This questionnaire relates to McGregor's motivational theories, where the 'X' manager believes in beating the donkey with a stick, whereas the 'Y' manager believes in encouraging with a carrot. Place your total score on the line below.

X type
(9 points)

Y type
(45 points)

In this section we are focusing on P3, P4, P5, P6, M3, M4 and D2 from Unit 5 – 'Understanding Discipline within the Uniformed Public Services'.

These grading criteria cover two key themes: conformity and obedience P3, P4, M3 (both theoretical studies of these issues and their application in the uniformed public services) and concepts of different types of authority, authority in uniformed public services and issues that arise when there is a lack of discipline P5, P6, M4.

D2 then brings those themes together in an evaluation of issues around blind obedience to authority.

Uniformed public services are unique in their need to have clearly defined authority and staff trained to follow and obey orders, but blind obedience can have devastating consequences if authority is imposed inappropriately.

Inspector of Prisons, HM Chief Inspector of Fire Services; extent of authority; power or right to enforce obedience

Nature of authority: power; position; status; influence; corruption; disobedience; blind obedience including both positive and negative aspects; moral dilemmas and responsibility for decisions taken

Types of authority: authoritarian; dictatorial; consultative; participative; how these forms of authority are applied to the uniformed public services

Legislation: eg Armed Forces Discipline Act 2000; Police and Criminal Evidence Act 1984 (Section IX); Police Act 1997 (Section 50); Fire and Rescue Services Act 2004, including any subsequent amendments.

Content

2) **Know what conformity and obedience mean, highlighting their place in the uniformed public services**

   Conformity: compliance with common practices; social norms; the role of self esteem; the purpose of uniforms; the relevance of conformity in the uniformed public services

   Obedience: as an act, practice or quality; following orders; conscious and unconscious obedience; compliance; status as a factor in obedience; influences, eg fear, reward, love, respect; the relevance of obedience in the uniformed public services

   Research studies: eg Asch, Milgram, Hoffling, Zimbardo.

4) **Know the complex nature of authority in the uniformed public services**

   Authority: within a range of different uniformed public services, eg Independent Police Complaints Commission, HM Chief

Grading Criteria

P3 explain what is meant by conformity and obedience, and how they are represented in the uniformed public services, including the factors that influence them

P4 describe three research studies which explore conformity and obedience

M3 analyse how three research studies on conformity and obedience apply to the uniformed services

To achieve these criteria you will need to investigate what the terms 'obedience' and 'conformity' actually mean and also the research that has been conducted on the themes of conformity and obedience (use the unit content above as guidance). You will need to apply these concepts in a uniformed public services context.

P5 describe four types of authority

P6 explain the nature of authority in relation to the uniformed public services

M4 explain the importance of recognising authority and the consequences of a lack of authority within the uniformed public services

For these grading criteria you will need to understand the different types of authority that exist and how and why authority is exercised in uniformed public services. You will also need to explain what happens when there is a lack of authority in a uniformed public service context.

D2 critically evaluate the positive and negative effects of blind obedience to authority

Whilst it is important to ensure that staff in uniformed public services follow instructions and conform to organisational norms and values, if authority is misused or applied inappropriately, the consequences can be enormous. To achieve this grading criteria you will need to look at both the positive and negative aspects of obedience and then review the arguments for and against blind obedience and the use and misuse of authority.

Case study 1 – Conformity and rules

Conformity is the process by which people's beliefs or behaviours are influenced by others. People can be influenced via subtle, even unconscious processes, or by direct and overt peer pressure. Conformity can have either good or bad effects on people, from driving safely on the correct side of the road, to harmful drug or alcohol abuse.

Conformity is a group behaviour. Numerous factors, such as group size, unanimity, cohesion, status, prior commitment and public opinion all help to determine the level of conformity an individual will reflect towards his or her group. Conformity influences the formation and maintenance of social norms.

Source: http://en.wikipedia.org/wiki/Conformity_(psychology)

When we are conforming we are acting in accordance with regulations, rules and authority.

We are complying with the norms and practices of organisations and societies.

- Consider the following discussion:

Sam and Becky were discussing rules and regulations. When they'd been at school they had to follow rules such as getting to school on time, wearing uniform (and making sure they looked smart), doing homework and handing it in on time, behaving properly.

Now they were at college they had to follow similar rules. There wasn't a uniform, but there was an expectation of being dressed appropriately, especially when they had visitors in to speak to the class or went on visits and trips, like last week when they'd visited the Magistrates' Courts for their Law Unit.

Then they discussed what the students did wear to college and decided they had imposed their own uniform because almost all the class wore jeans, sweatshirts and trainers!

They were also expected to behave well, to obey the rules in the college handbook and attend all their lessons on time. Then there were assignments! They both knew that if these were late they would get a yellow card and if the second deadline was missed, a red card and a discipline interview with the Head of Department! Oh yes! They also had to reference all their work and acknowledge sources, including the Internet, or else!

At home there were even more rules but these varied depending on how strict their parents were or how well (or badly) they had behaved in the past! (Home rules included things like what time to get up, when to come home, keeping bedrooms tidy, asking before inviting friends round, going for Sunday lunch at Gran's, taking turns to do washing up.)

The class had been asked to agree their own group rules for the residential they were going on and so far had agreed on:

- Respect yourself and others
- Listen and don't interrupt others
- Don't be afraid to ask for help if you need it
- Timekeeping is important.

Some definitions

Obedience vs conformity, both involve social pressure	
Conformity	Obedience
pressure from group norm (equal status)	pressure from instruction (hierarchy) likely to involve public behaviour only

Conformity is a type of social influence involving a change in belief or behaviour in order to fit in with a group. This change is in response to real (involving the physical presence of others) or imagined (involving the pressure of social norms/expectations) group pressure. Conformity can also be simply defined as 'conformity to group pressures'. Group pressure may take different forms, for example bullying, persuasion, teasing, criticism etc. Conformity is also known as majority influence. The term is often used to indicate an agreement to the majority position, brought about either by a desire to 'fit in' (normative) or because of uncertainty with one's own position (informational), or simply to conform to a social role (internalisation).

Man (1969) states that 'the essence of conformity is yielding to group pressure'.

He distinguished between four different types of conformity:

1) **Normative:** yielding to group pressure because a person wants to fit in with the group. Conforming because the person is scared of being rejected by the group. This was demonstrated by the Asch Study. This type of conformity usually involves compliance — where a person publicly accepts the views of a group but privately rejects them.

2) **Informational:** this usually occurs when a person lacks knowledge and looks to the group for guidance. Or when a person is in an

ambiguous (or unclear) situation and socially compares their behaviour with the group. This type of conformity usually involves internalisation – where a person accepts the views of the group and adopts them as an individual, eg a non-Muslim visitor to a mosque removing shoes or a visitor to a Catholic Church covering their shoulders.

3) **Compliance:** publicly changing behaviour to fit in with the group while privately disagreeing. In other words, conforming to the majority (publicly) in spite of not really agreeing with them (privately). This is seen in Asch's line experiment.

4) **Internalisation:** publicly changing behaviour to fit in with the group and also agreeing with them privately.

There are also other types of conformity.

5) **Ingratiational:** where a person conforms to impress or gain favour/ acceptance from other people. It is similar to normative influence but is motivated by the need for social rewards rather than the threat of rejection, ie group pressure does not enter the decision to conform.

6) **Non-conformity:** this may amount to either (i) independence of behaviour, or (ii) anti-conformity, which amounts to rebellion against group norms for its own sake.

ACTIVITY 1

Working in teams of four or five, consider the following issues:

a) Find some definitions or explanations for the following terms:

- Social norms
- Peer pressure
- Unanimity
- Group cohesion
- Status
- Self esteem
- Compliance.

Produce a poster to display these definitions.

b) Either as a whole class or in teams related to teamwork activities you are undertaking, devise your own group rules. Aim for about ten things you can all agree on.

Write these up on a flip chart for reference.

Now decide how you will enforce those rules.

Who will take responsibility for challenging breaches of the rules?

Will there be any sanctions for those who break the rules or rewards for those who keep them?

c) What rules govern your conduct at school/college?

Do you agree with these?

Why do you think they exist? What's their purpose?

How are these communicated to you?

Is there a handbook or learner contract?

What are the sanctions for those who break the rules?

Are there any rewards for keeping the rules?

What happens if people refuse to follow the rules (i) in college or school or (ii) in society?

d) Agree with your teacher which specific uniformed public service your group will investigate.

Find out what rules govern the behaviour of personnel in that specific service.

For example, the conduct of police officers comes under the police code of conduct which you can find at www.ipcc.gov.uk/index/complainants/who_complaint/pol_codeconduct.htm.

All organisations which employ staff in the UK are required by law to have a discipline policy and this will summarise behaviour that would be seen to be breaching the organisation's rules on conduct. You can find out more at www.acas.org.uk/index.aspx?articleid=896.

- Produce a PowerPoint presentation summarising your findings for sections c) and d) and deliver this to the rest of your class.

ACTIVITY 2

THE PURPOSE OF UNIFORMS

Why do some members of public services wear uniforms? Police forces in the UK employ a wide range of staff for a number of different functions and roles. These staff can be divided into uniformed and non-uniformed, but that division could be misleading. The personnel who usually wear uniforms are Police Officers (or Constables), Special Constables and Community Support Officers (CSOs). Some police officers (such as plain clothes detectives and undercover officers) do not wear uniforms.

In the Prison Service uniformed staff are the Prison Officers, Senior Officers, Principal Officers and Officer Support Grades (OSGs). Increasingly, senior management wear suits rather than uniforms. In Juvenile and Young Offender Institutions there has been a move to encourage officers to exchange the traditional navy blue uniform for track suits. The rationale behind this is that it may help young offenders to relate to staff better and remove barriers, but some officers have been reluctant to comply with this trend.

Working in groups of three or four:

a) Produce a mind map showing all the possible reasons your group can think of for personnel in the public services wearing uniforms. What are the advantages and disadvantages of wearing a uniform? Display your mind map on a piece of flip chart paper.

b) Individually, ask members of uniformed public services how they feel about wearing their uniform. Do they feel proud? Do they have a sense of belonging?

As a whole class:

c) Discuss why you think prison officers might be reluctant to comply with the move from their 'blues' to track suits and polo shirts?

d) Consider this situation. A member of senior management was visiting a prison where he did not work and was wearing a suit. As he crossed the exercise yard there was a fight and Prison Officers were summoned by the alarm bell to deal with the situation. The senior manager got caught up in it all and ended up quite badly injured – the staff had not recognised him as prison service personnel and neither had the prisoners.

What do you think are the key issues from this story? How might this example influence the situation described in c) above?

Case study 2 – Police to wear uniforms at Pride

Officers from Sussex Police are to march in uniform at the Gay Pride parade in Brighton on Saturday – for the first time. The Deputy Chief Constable said the rule had been relaxed for all events attended by the Gay Police Association (GPA). Sussex officers have to seek permission but Hampshire police have been told they are not allowed to wear uniforms. Sussex Police said it hoped the move would help reflect the large lesbian, gay, bisexual and trans gendered community served by the force.

Last year, uniformed officers from across the UK were among 60,000 people to take part in the Gay Pride parade held in London. The Deputy Chief Constable said he hoped the move would have 'a positive impact on the confidence the lesbian, gay, bisexual and trans gendered community has in Sussex Police'. The GPA said: 'Officers marching in uniform... demonstrates that not only do officers police the lesbian, gay, bisexual and trans gendered community, but they are also part of that community themselves and not ashamed to publicly show this.' Forces in the neighbouring counties of Hampshire and Surrey had a mixed response to the invitation by Sussex Police for their officers to join the parade in uniform. Hampshire's Chief Constable said he would not allow off-duty officers to do so. 'It is my view that participation in uniform could undermine the traditional neutrality of the police service,' he said.

Source: http://news.bbc.co.uk/nolpda/ukfs_news/hi/newsid_3541000/3541510.stm

6 August 2004

Navy lets sailors march at Gay Pride, 25 June 2006

Military officials have given the go-ahead for gay and lesbian naval personnel to march in full uniform for the first time at Britain's annual Gay Pride celebrations. More than 40 sailors, from able seamen to Royal Navy Reserve commanders, will lead the EuroPride parade through London. The Navy said it was the first time that any military organisation in the world had allowed gay and lesbian recruits to march in uniform at such an event. 'They will not be marching in a parade formation but they will be walking smartly and in full uniform with medals,' said the Navy's diversity spokesman.

Source: http://news.independent.co.uk/

ACTIVITY 3

a) The examples in the case study show different views of when it is appropriate for personnel from the public services to wear uniforms and when it isn't.

As a class, discuss the different points of view and see if you can decide the reasons for these different perspectives.

b) Why do organisations like St John's Ambulance and the Salvation Army wear uniforms?

c) An off-duty Prison Officer stopped at a convenience store on her way home from work to buy a bottle of wine. The store owner refused to serve her saying it was against the law to sell alcohol to a Police Officer in uniform. She explained she was a Prison Officer and showed her HMPS ID, but the shop owner said it made no difference.

Find out if this is true. What are your views about personnel from any uniformed public service buying alcohol when wearing their uniform?

The 1964 Licensing Act may be a good place to begin!

Case study 3 – Perceptions of authority

Divine authority: all religions (Hinduism, Islam, Buddhism, Christianity and others) consider God as the supreme authority. All the religious scriptures have considered God to have authority and wisdom, which is far superior to that of humans. God is the creator and therefore superior to man. Divinity, as presented in religious scriptures, makes claim to the final authority for all truth and reality, and rules all of creation.

Max Weber considered that authority comprises a particular type of power. He defined authority as power which is recognised as legitimate and justified by both the powerful and the powerless. Weber divided authority into three types:

Traditional authority which simply derives from long-established customs, habits and social structures. Passing of power from one generation to another is an example of traditional authority, eg the right of hereditary monarchs to rule.

Rational-legal authority is that form of authority which depends for its legitimacy on formal rules, which are usually written down, and are often very complex. Their powers are usually mentioned in the constitution of the state and in the nation's laws and legal systems. Modern societies depend on legal-rational authority. Personnel in uniformed public services are good examples.

In **Charismatic** authority, the charisma or personal influence of the individual or the leader plays an important role. Charismatic authority suggests that the authority of the charismatic ruler is superior to the validity of both traditional and rational-legal authority. Followers accept this and are willing to follow this higher or inspired authority in the place of the authority that they have followed in the past.

History has witnessed social movements and revolution against a system of traditional or legal-rational authority, which are usually started by Charismatic authority. The careers of Lenin, Hitler and Lech Wał sa can be considered in this regard. Charismatic authority never lasts long (even when successful). It has a short span of life and it inevitably gives way to either traditional or to legal-rational authority which are more time tested and sustaining in the long run.

What distinguishes authority from coercion, force and power on one hand and leadership, persuasion and influence on the other hand is **legitimacy**. Those ruling feel that they have a right to issue commands; those being ruled perceive an obligation to obey. Authority is one of several resources available to holders of formal positions. A Head of State is dependent upon authority. Legitimacy must be acknowledged not just by citizens but by those who control other valued resources: staff, cabinet, military leaders and the administrative, legal and political structures of the entire society.

Source: http://en.wikipedia.org/wiki/Authority/

ACTIVITY 4

DEFINITIONS OF AUTHORITY

Case study 3 describes divine authority, traditional authority, rational-legal authority and charismatic authority.

Other definitions are authoritarian, dictatorial, consultative and participative.

These definitions may overlap – for example charismatic authority may also be dictatorial.

In small groups agree with your teacher which of these four definitions of authority (authoritarian, dictatorial, consultative and participative) you will research.

■ Find out what the definition means and any examples of the use of that type of authority.

■ Explain when (if ever) this type of authority would be used in uniformed public services.

■ What are the positive aspects of this type of authority and what are the negatives of its use?

■ Each group should produce a fact sheet explaining the specific type of authority in relation to the uniformed public services.

ACTIVITY 5

AUTHORITY IN UNIFORMED PUBLIC SERVICES

In Unit 1 you examined the roles of the various Inspectorates eg Independent Police Complaints Commission (IPCC), HM Chief Inspector of Prisons (HMCIP), HM Chief Inspector of Fire Services, Health Care Commission.

In groups, select one of these bodies and research the extent of its authority and its power or right to enforce obedience.

If, for example, HMCIP found that conditions in a specific prison were unacceptable, what powers do they have to enforce change? If the IPCC uphold a complaint against the police what authority does it have to enforce change or initiate disciplinary actions?

Produce a poster explaining the extent of the authority of your chosen Inspectorate and its powers to enforce obedience.

ACTIVITY 6

LEGISLATION WHICH CONFERS AUTHORITY

Uniformed public service	Relevant legislation	What powers and authority this confers
Police	Police & Criminal Evidence Act 1984	
	Police Act 1997 (section 50)	
	Police Reform Act 2002	
Prisons	The Prison (Amendment) Rules 2005	
Fire & Rescue Services	Fire and Rescue Services Act 2004	
Armed Forces	Armed Forces Discipline Act 2000	
	Armed Forces Act 2006	

Copy the table. Working in small groups, research the legislation and then complete your table.

ACTIVITY 7

WHAT IS OBEDIENCE TO AUTHORITY?

Obedience is the performance of an action in response to a direct order. Usually the order comes from a person of high status or authority such as parents, teachers, doctors, the police (Franzoi 1996).

For many years, psychologists have been carrying out research into why we obey authority (both in a personal and organisational context). The table overleaf details some of the most interesting research and the case studies on the following pages give some detail about these research studies. Because of the ethical issues raised it is unlikely these studies would be allowed to be undertaken now!

Ethical considerations eg Milgram:

- **Consent** – not informed. Participants volunteered for a learning experiment, not one on obedience.
- **Deception** – as to nature of experiment. Shocks not real. Victim not really a participant.
- **Protection of participants** – the participants displayed symptoms similar to that of a nervous breakdown.
- **Withdrawal from the investigation** – physically the participants could withdraw but with strong social pressure on them this was unlikely. The prods used, such as 'you have no alternative, you must go on', ensured this.
- **Observation** – participants were filmed without their consent.

Research study	Main issue researched	
Asch 1951, 1956	The influence of the majority	Case study 4
Milgram 1963	Obedience	Case study 5
Hofling 1966	Nurses and obedience	Case study 6
Meeus and Raajmakers 1995	Obedience in job interviews	Case study 7
Moscovici 1969	The influence of the minority	Case study 8
Zimbardo 1973	Stanford Prison experiment	Case study 9
	Blind obedience	Case study 10

- Divide into small groups and agree which of the research studies you will investigate, using the case studies (4–9) as your starting point.
- Find out how the research was conducted, what the key finding were and evaluate the study in terms of the ethical considerations listed above.
- Use Case study 10 to extend your research and to critically evaluate the positive and negative effects of blind obedience to authority.
- Produce a slide show, and deliver it to the rest of the class, which describes your chosen research study and analyses how it could be applied to the uniformed public services and critically evaluates the positive and negative effects of blind obedience to authority.

Case study 4 – Asch

Asch believed people wouldn't go along with the crowd; he set up his experiment to prove that people would stand up against group pressure. Unknown to his subjects, the rest of the group were stooges or plants, who'd been instructed to say A was longer than B, even though it patently wasn't. Contrary to his expectations, Asch discovered that a third of people went along with the group, even when it contradicted the evidence of their own eyes.

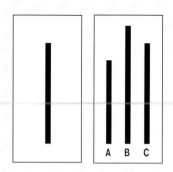

The participants (who were unaware of the experiment) were presented with an unambiguous line judgement task. Participants were presented with two cards. One had on it a 'standard' line. On the other were three comparison lines. They were asked to judge which of the comparison lines were equal in length to the standard line. This was done with a control group of 37 people, where the pressure to conform was removed. It was also done with an experimental group containing 6–8 confederates briefed in advance by Asch and one naïve participant, who was second to last to answer. At first the confederates gave the correct answer, then they changed to giving the same unanimous wrong answer.

In the control group 35 of the participants made no errors, one made a single error. Only 0.7 per cent of the judgements were incorrect. In the experimental groups 37 per cent of the judgements were incorrect. Of the 125 participants, only 25 per cent gave the correct answer every time, compared to the 95 per cent result from the control group.

This was clearly a case of normative social influence, as participants did not want to 'stand out like a sore thumb' or 'rock the boat', risking group disapproval. It was a case of public compliance. The power of majority influence was shown.

Because it was an unambiguous task, it showed clearly public acceptance from normative social influence rather than informational influence. However, it lacked external validity. This situation was artificial and unlikely to occur in everyday life, therefore the participants acted in a different way to how they would usually act and the results could not be generalised to the real world.

Source: www.qeliz.ac.uk/psychology/Asch.htm

Case study 5 – Milgram and obedience

Controversy surrounded Stanley Milgram for much of his professional life as a result of a series of experiments on obedience to authority which he conducted at Yale University in 1961–1962. He found, surprisingly, that 65 per cent of his subjects, ordinary residents of New Haven, were willing to give apparently harmful electric shocks – up to 450 volts – to a pitifully protesting victim, simply because a scientific authority commanded them to, and in spite of the fact that the victim did not do anything to deserve such punishment. The victim was, in reality, a good actor who did not actually receive shocks, and this fact was revealed to the subjects at the end of the experiment. But, during the experiment itself, the experience was a powerfully real and gripping one for most participants.

Who are more obedient – men or women? Milgram found an identical rate of obedience in both groups – 65 per cent – although obedient women consistently reported more stress than men. There are about a dozen replications of the obedience experiment world-wide which had male and female subjects. All of them, with one exception, also found no male–female differences.

Source: www.stanleymilgram.com

Milgram Different conditions

Condition volt shock	What happened	% gave 450
Remote feedback	Victim not heard/seen	66%
Voice feedback	Victim heard/not seen	62%
Proximity	Victim 1 metre from participant	40%
Touch-proximity	As above, but participant forced victim's hand onto shock plate	30%

Case study 6 – Hofling, nurses and obedience

Throughout our youth we obey people in a position of authority, our parents, teachers and other 'grown-ups'. However, as we mature and reach adulthood, do we still conform and comply with authority? And does this 'obedience' continue throughout our careers?

Several studies have been undertaken throughout the years to determine just how far human nature will go to comply with authority. One of the most well-known with regards to nursing is Hofling et al. (1966). The aim of the study was to discover if a nurse would intentionally cause harm to a patient if a doctor ordered her to.

Hofling met with nurses on 22 different wards to warn them of the dangers of a new drug, Astroten, and its extreme toxicity. (Astroten was actually a fictitious drug made up by the researchers and was nothing more than glucose.) Later, he asked a doctor whom the nurses knew to be on the staff but had never met, to call each of the wards. The doctor asked that 20 mg of Astroten be given to a patient. Despite having been told that the maximum dose for this drug was 10 mg, and against hospital policy which clearly stated drugs cannot be prescribed over the phone, 21 out of the 22 nurses administered or attempted to administer the drug. Even the fact that

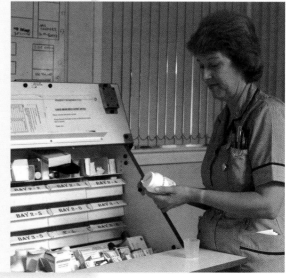

the drug was not on the ward stock list clearing it for use did not prevent these nurses from choosing to follow a 'doctor's' orders.

In another study by Krackow and Blass (1995), 46 per cent of registered nurses admitted to complying with a doctor's order that they felt was unsafe. Five hundred questionnaires were sent out to nurses which included questions about the last time they had refused to carry out a physician's orders because they felt it was unsafe. Only a little over half of the nurses questioned said they had refused the doctor's orders. The nurses involved in the Hofling study later reported that they had followed the doctor's orders because they had experienced a doctor's wrath when they had questioned an order before.

As students, most nurses will follow an authoritative figure's order without question. As we progress and become more confident we are more likely to question something. However, as the study by Krackow and Blass shows, even by today's standards, nurses will still not always stand up for themselves and ultimately, their patients. They suggest that physicians are seen as authority and, as Lutsky (1995) says 'When an individual acts consistently with authorized command, instruction, or rule, he/she is commonly described as being obedient to authority'.

Source: www.nursesnetwork.co.uk/forum/index.php?showtopic=1263

Conclusion: in their roles as nurses, it is the social norm to accept orders from the higher authority of the doctors without questioning their judgement. This shows that obedience is commonplace in everyday life.

Evaluation: it was unethical. Participants did not have the opportunity to give informed consent as they did not know that they were participating in an experiment.

This experiment shows the importance of responsibility in relation to obedience. As the doctor claimed that he would sign the authorisation papers when he arrived, the responsibility was removed from the nurses, making them more likely to obey.

The drug that the nurses were asked to administer was one that was unknown to them. When the experiment was repeated with a drug that the nurses had heard of not one of them obeyed.

Case study 7 – Meeus + Raajmaker's study of obedience in a job interview (1986)

Aims: to investigate obedience in a real life situation (job interview) where people had the time to think about the situation and their actions.

Procedures: 24 Dutch participants were asked to interview applicants for a job. Unknown to the participants, the applicants were confederates. Holland had a high unemployment rate at the time of this experiment, so failing the interview would have been disastrous to the applicants. At various points in the interview participants were asked to make 'stress remarks', for example, 'If you continue like this you'll fail the test', or 'This job is too difficult for you. You are more suited to lower functions.' Participants were told that the job required people who could handle stress, so the remarks were necessary.

There were 15 stress remarks, each increasing in severity. Participants were instructed to make all of the remarks, no matter how much the applicants complained. If they halted, they were prodded by the experimenter. At the start of the interview applicants appeared confident and at ease. They became increasingly distressed as the interview went on. They complained that the remarks were ruining their chance of getting a job and got very angry. By the end of the interview they were in a state of despair.

Findings: despite finding the interview distasteful, unfair and humiliating to the applicants, 22/24 of the participants made all of the remarks. This was the result in the group with the authority figure (experimenter) present. In a control group where there was no authority figure, none of the participants made all of the remarks.

Conclusion: this experiment shows that obedience studies are applicable to real life situations. As results from a further study show (where participants were given one week's notice of the interview with full details of what they were expected to do), still 22/24 of the participants made all of the stress remarks. This indicates that having time to consider their actions did not have any bearing on the obedience rate.

This study was conducted when the rate of unemployment was high in Holland. This obviously affected the results. So we must ask would the same results be found if the study was carried out today?

Source: www.qeliz.ac.uk/Psychology/Meeus + Raajmakers1987.htm

Research further at: www.ycc.ac.uk/yc/new/HUMSOC/psycho/unit3/Word/meeusraaj.doc

Case study 8 – Moscovici – minority influence

Moscovici claimed that majority influence in many ways was misleading – if the majority was indeed all-powerful, we would all end up thinking the same. He pointed to the fact that most major social movements have been started by individuals and small groups (eg Christianity, Buddhism, the Suffragette movement, Nazism, etc) and that without an outspoken minority, we would have no innovation or social change. The study he is most famous for, influences of a consistent minority on the responses of a majority in a colour perception task, is now seen as one of the defining investigations into the effects of minority influence.

Aims: to investigate how a consistent minority affect the opinions of a larger group (majority) possibly creating doubt and leading them (the majority) to question and alter their views.

Procedures: thirty-two groups of six participants were shown coloured blue slides of varying shades. Two of the participants were in fact confederates (stooges) of Moscovici and had been instructed to consistently describe the slides as green. The remaining participants were asked to say what colour they judged the slides to be.

Findings: for 8.42 per cent of the trials, participants agreed with the minority and said that the slides were green. Overall, 32 per cent of the participants agreed at least once.

Conclusions: the study suggested that minorities can indeed exert an effect over the opinion of a majority. Not to the same degree as majority influence, but the fact that almost a third of people agreed at least once is significant. However, this also leaves two thirds who never agreed. In a follow up-experiment, Moscovici demonstrated that consistency was the key factor in minority influence. By instructing the stooges to be inconsistent, the effect fell off sharply.

Case study 9 – Abuse At Iraqi Prison Predictable, Decades-Old Study Shows 05.27.2004

It's 2:30 a.m. Bored prison guards pull prisoners from their cells, strip them naked, chain them together and humiliate them. The guards know someone is recording their activities, but they don't let concerns about future consequences interfere with the degradation and abuse.

Sound familiar? It might sound like abuses that occurred at Abu Ghraib prison in Baghdad, but these pictures were taken over 30 years ago – at Stanford University.

In 1971 a group of 24 college men volunteered to act as either guards or prisoners in an experimental prison. Under the watchful eye of Dr Philip Zimbardo, volunteers went through several rounds of testing to ensure psychological and physical health and 'normalcy.' They were then designated either guards or prisoners by the simple flip of a coin.

Two days into the experiment, the normal, adjusted students were playing their prison roles with frightening reality. The 'prisoners,' fed up with having roll calls in the middle of the night, rebelled by pushing their beds against their cell bars and refusing to come out. The 'guards' called in reinforcements, pulled the prisoners from their cells, striped them naked, and proceeded to humiliate and abuse them for hours. To further reinforce their power, the guards took away bathroom privileges. It got worse – so bad that Zimbardo halted the planned two-week study after only six days.

Fast forward to the Abu Ghraib prison scandal and Zimbardo sees a connection. While American officials have been blaming the situation on 'a few bad apples,' Zimbardo told MTV News it's more like 'a bad barrel converting good apples into bad apples.'

'When people are deindividualised, they are usually put in herds, or groups, and given numbers. Their identity is taken away,' Zimbardo said. '[In Abu Ghraib] the guards had a mob mentality, a group mindset. You start to do things because other people in your group are doing them.' Psychologists call it the 'Lord of the Flies' effect, named for William Golding's book, in which he describes the transformation of shipwrecked, island-bound English choirboys into a murderous mob.

Zimbardo went on to explain that the Stanford prison experiment and the Abu Ghraib prison scandal were built on the same foundations with similar (and even predictable) results. Inexperienced guards were given little instruction, extraordinary power and limited oversight. In Abu Ghraib that dynamic was heightened by the stress of war and death and the need for information from Iraqi prisoners.

Source: www.mtv.com/chooseorlose/headlines/news.jhtml?id=1487984

Site for Zimbardo – Stanford Prison Experiment: www.prisonexp.org

INDIVIDUAL ACTIVITY – QUIZ

1) What was the rate of conformity in the control group in Asch's line experiment?

a	b	c	d
0.7%	37%	1.85%	24%

2) In Hofling's experiment of obedience in a hospital, how many nurses were involved?

a	b	c	d
21	22	20	17

3) In Meeus and Raajmaker's study of obedience, how many participants made all of the stress remarks after they had had a week before the interview to consider their actions?

a	b	c	d
20/24	22/24	23/25	22/25

4) What was the conformity rate in Moscovici's study of minority influence in the inconsistent group?

a	b	c	d
8.25	8.42%	1.25%	0.25%

5) In Zimbardo's prison experiment, how many participants began a hunger strike?

a	b	c	d
6	1	5	4

6) How many orders were given to the 'teacher' in Milgram's experiment when they refused to give shocks?

a	b	c	d
5	15	2	4

7) What did one of the 'prisoners' suffer in Zimbardo's prison experiment?

a	b	c	d
A psychosomatic rash	A seizure	A severe headache	A beating from the officers

8) In Milgram's experiment when there were two confederates joining the 'teacher' who rebelled against the experimenter, what was the obedience rate?

a	b	c	d
10%	37%	48%	30%

9) What percentage of the control group gave the correct answer every time in Asch's line experiment?

a	b	c	d
37%	95%	90%	63%

10) In Moscovici's minority influence study, what percentage of participants agreed at least once that the slides were green?

a	b	c	d
25%	8.42%	32%	67%

Source: www.qeliz.ac.uk/psychology/quiz

Case study 10

Blind obedience is a virtue only in a very few circumstances. It's perfectly arguable that being an adult at all means having the capacity to ask awkward questions about the right of others to tell us what to do, so that the child's challenge is itself a mark of growing up. But one of the most sensitive areas for awkward questions is our relation with law and government.

Why should we do what the government tells us? It's a question that takes us into some unexpectedly complicated areas. It raises issues about the unspoken contracts that people feel exist between themselves and their rulers. You need to be reasonably confident that your system of government is worth supporting overall if you're prepared to go along with what it tells you in some particular areas where you may not feel convinced or are frankly not convinced at all. It's the problem that political thinkers describe as the legitimacy of a system – it's 'right' to order you around.

The Richard Dimbleby Lecture 2002, 'Nations, markets and morals'

Archbishop of Canterbury, Dr Rowan Williams

Some examples of blind obedience:

- **The Holocaust:** blind obedience carried to the extreme. In World War II the Nazis established death camps where soldiers and even prisoners obeyed commands to systematically murder millions of innocent victims. Orders were to be obeyed at all cost, without question, and the penalty for non-obedience in many cases was death. German participants in the Third Reich at first had difficulty with the utterly blind obedience required but facing death for disobedience, the principle became a defence mechanism allowing many to commit abominable acts and pass responsibility on to their superiors who in turn passed culpability upwards. In the end, no one was ultimately responsible, as the leadership would claim they had no idea what was going on while the underlings claimed 'orders from above'. (See: http://shoaheducation.com/)
- **Tiananmen Square** China 4 June 1989: the willingness of Chinese troops to fire on unarmed civilians during a peaceful demonstration and later search out and kill those who had been involved and then fled from the scene.
- **Robert Maxwell** undoubtedly behaved in a highly unethical and socially irresponsible manner. Described as a 'bully' by many who worked with him, Maxwell was, at the same time, a highly charismatic individual; a leader who demanded blind obedience in his followers and that blind obedience led to the collapse of Maxwell's empire. (See: www.caledoniancrag.com/documents/ISBEE Drennan paper.doc)
- **Abu Ghraib prison 2003**.
- **'Ethnic cleansing' in Kosovo**.
- **My Lai massacre**, which took place on the morning of March 16, 1968: a watershed in the history of modern American combat.

Answers to the quiz

Q1	0.7%
Q2	22
Q3	22 out of 24
Q4	1.25%
Q5	1
Q6	4
Q7	A psychosomatic rash
Q8	10%
Q9	95%
Q10	32%

95

UNIT 7 – PHYSICAL PREPARATION AND FITNESS FOR THE UNIFORMED SERVICES

In this section we are focusing on P2, P4, M2, M3 and D1 from Unit 7 – 'Physical Preparation and Fitness for the Uniformed Services'.

Content

2) **Understand the effects of lifestyle factors on health and fitness**

Lifestyle factors: physical activity; smoking; alcohol; drugs (recreational, performance enhancing); stress; diet (requirements, recommendations, nutrition); personal hygiene

Effects: physical activity, eg physical and psychological health benefits, social benefits; smoking, eg physical health risks; alcohol, eg physical and psychological health risks; drugs, eg physical and mental health effects, policies of the uniformed public services; stress, eg physical and mental health risks; post-traumatic stress disorder; diet, eg benefits of healthy diet; effects of poor nutrition; personal hygiene (infections while on uniformed public service operations); importance of body weight, eg entry to the uniformed public services.

3) **Be able to plan a fitness training programme to prepare for uniformed public service**

Components of fitness: health related (aerobic capacity, strength, muscular endurance, flexibility, body composition); skill-related (speed, reaction time, agility, balance, coordination, power)

Training programme: goals (specific to individual, related to requirements of specific uniformed public service); fitness tests (appropriate to uniformed public services); principles of training (overload, specificity, progression, variation, reversibility, FITT principles – frequency, intensity, time, type); periodisation (macrocycle, mesocycle, microcycle); training techniques, eg resistance training, continuous training, interval training, circuit training; training diary, eg progression, attitude, motivation, linked to goals.

Grading Criteria

P2 describe the lifestyle factors that can affect health and fitness, and the effects they can have

M2 explain the effects that lifestyle factors can have on health and fitness, when applying for a uniformed public service and long-term employment

D1 evaluate the effects that lifestyle factors can have on health and fitness, when applying for a uniformed public service and long-term employment

To achieve these criteria you will need to understand how lifestyle factors impact on health and fitness. You will also need to understand why a good level of health and fitness is important both when applying to join a uniformed public service and throughout your career in the uniformed public services.

P4 plan a personal fitness training programme to prepare for a selected uniformed public service, with support from others

M3 plan a personal fitness training programme to prepare for uniformed public service

These grading criteria require you to design a personal fitness training programme for your own fitness development. To do this you will first need to decide which uniformed service you wish to join and then undertake an assessment of your current fitness level against the fitness entry requirements and job-related requirements for the chosen service.

You will then need to plan your training programme to ensure that it enables you to develop the specific areas of fitness required eg strength, stamina, flexibility etc. requires you to develop a suitable programme with assistance. For M3 you should be able to do this by yourself.

UNIT ACTIVITIES

You will undertake a range of activities in this introduction to Unit 7 which will all lead to planning and undertaking a 'well-being' activity or exhibition for your school or college to benefit both other students and all the staff who form part of your school/college community.

You may also think about opening up this activity or exhibition to parents, other members of the local community or other schools in your area.

Case study 1 – Positive support for 'staff well-being' days – 2 March 2005

The Prison Service's Staff Fitness Testing Team have been working in partnership with the HMYOI Glen Parva and HMP Birmingham to introduce staff 'well-being' events promoting general health and wellness. This is a very positive new development as part of the Prison Service's wider occupational health strategy.

Activities and contributions to the 'well-being' event were made from a variety of internal and external sources. These included the fitness team's 'Body MOT' consisting of blood pressure check, body fat weight monitor, Spirometer (lung and carbon monoxide test) and a cholesterol check. The day also included advice on smoking cessation, managing stress, walking for life, nutrition and healthy eating and alcohol and drug abuse support. Over 180 staff from Glen Parva and Birmingham participated in the events and both were strongly supported by the respective Governors and proved to be very popular with staff.

Commenting on this new programme the Director of Personnel, said: 'The fitness testing team will offer one well-being event per month throughout the coming year. I see this initiative building upon and supporting the excellent work already being carried out by Occupational Health Advisors and PE staff in prisons.'

Source: www.hmprisonservice.gov.uk/news/latestnews/index.asp?id=2611,38,6,38,0,0

Absence from the workplace

In 2006 absence levels in the public services decreased to 4.3 per cent of working time lost (9.9 days per employee) from 4.5 per cent for 2005. Manufacturing and production employers report a reduction in average absence levels to 3.6 per cent (8.2 days per employee) from 3.7 per cent last year.

Stress is reported as a key factor in short term absence from work by 82 per cent of public services workers and in long term absence by 52 per cent.

Source: CIPD Survey report 'Absence Management' July 2006.

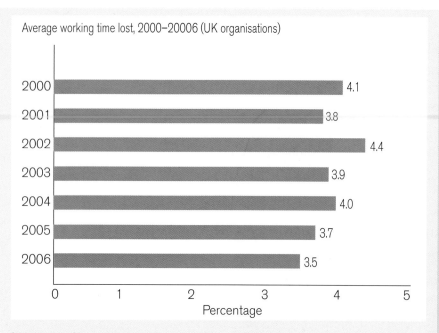

Average working time lost, 2000–20006 (UK organisations)

Year	Percentage
2000	4.1
2001	3.8
2002	4.4
2003	3.9
2004	4.0
2005	3.7
2006	3.5

Initiatives used by organisations to support employee well-being

	Total	Manufacturing and production	Private services	Non-profit organisations	Publiic services
Advice on healthy eating	25	29	18	15	40
Healthy menu in eployee canteen	25	28	20	17	37
Healthy snacks in vending machine	13	21	10	1	11
In-house-gym	12	7	9	8	27
Subsidised gym membership	28	21	30	25	43
Exercise classes provided on work premises	9	4	6	7	25
Support to stop smoking	34	40	21	31	57
Regular health checks	28	40	18	17	30
Private health insurance	60	71	77	31	12
Personalised healthy living programmes for employees	2	2	2	1	5
Employee assistance programme	32	25	32	47	40
Access to councelling service	55	49	46	62	87
Stress risk assessment	25	23	20	29	44
Access to physiotherapy	21	26	12		

Source: The CIPD Absence Management Survey (2006), with the permission of the publisher, the Chartered Institute of Personnel and Development, London (www.cipd.co.uk).

ACTIVITY 1

- Using Case study 1 and any other relevant examples, hold a class discussion on why a uniformed public service organisation like the prison service might hold 'well-being' days.

- In small groups find out the possible benefits to a uniformed public service organisation of raising staff awareness of health, lifestyle and nutrition.

- Why would the 'well-being' day offer a:
  - Blood pressure check

- Body fat and weight monitor
- Lung and carbon monoxide test
- Cholesterol check?

- Why do you think both the PE staff and Occupational Health were involved? What do Occupational Health do?

- The data above highlights the number of days lost to organisations through absence. The target for 2006/7 for the Prison Service is 12 days per employee. Review the data provided and any other information you can find and produce a short group presentation on the importance of health and fitness for employees in a uniformed public service.

Activity for your well-being exhibition/day

Each group (3 or 4 students) to produce a poster advertising the event in preparation to display in advance.

A useful guide to Health in the Workplace can be downloaded at: www.acas.org.uk/media/pdf/1/i/B11_1.pdf

---

Case study 2 – What is a healthy diet?

A healthy diet and keeping physically active can help to reduce the risk of developing heart disease. They can also increase chances of survival after a heart attack. What you eat and drink can affect the process of coronary heart disease by:

- Maintaining a healthy weight, reducing the strain on your heart
- Lowering your blood cholesterol level
- Keeping your blood pressure down
- Preventing atheroma (fatty material) inside your arteries
- Preventing blood clots forming.

Eating well offers many other health benefits. It can help protect against other conditions such as cancer and type 2 diabetes, and help you to maintain a healthy body weight.

Getting the balance right – A healthy diet contains plenty of fruit and vegetables and starchy foods such as wholegrain bread, pasta and rice; and is low in fat (especially saturated fat), salt and sugar.

Fruit and vegetables – There is good evidence that eating a diet that is rich in a range of vegetables and fruits lowers the risk of heart disease. Aim to eat at least five portions each day. They can be fresh, frozen, dried or tinned.

Fat and blood cholesterol – Reducing the total amount of fat you eat can help to reduce your blood cholesterol level. Too much saturated fat from fatty meats, biscuits, cakes and full fat dairy products can clog up your arteries and put a strain on your heart.

Oily fish – Eating oily fish regularly can help to reduce the risk of heart disease and improve the chances of survival after a heart attack. We do not know exactly how but the omega-3 fatty acids found in oily fish may keep the heartbeat regular, reduce triglyceride levels (these are fatty substances found in the blood) and prevent blood clots from forming in the coronary arteries.

Salt – Reducing the amount of salt you eat will also help keep your blood pressure down.

Alcohol – Too much alcohol can damage the heart muscle, increase blood pressure and also lead to weight gain. However, moderate drinking (between 1 and 2 units of alcohol a day) can help protect the heart in men aged over 40 and post-menopausal women.

Source: www.bhf.org.uk/keeping_your_heart_healthy/healthy_eating/what_is_a_healthy_diet.aspx

This item is reproduced with the kind permission of the British Heart Foundation, the copyright owner.

ACTIVITY 2

Divide into small groups and with the agreement of your tutor allocate the food groups between the groups (fruit and vegetables; starchy food (carbohydrates); fats; proteins).

Find out all you can about your food group, the types of food it includes, recommended daily intakes, the benefits from eating foods from this group and the issues that may arise from eating too much of your diet from a limited range of food groups.

Thinking about both informing your classmates and preparing for your well-being event, display the information your group has collected in one of the following formats:

- A short PowerPoint slide show
- An information leaflet
- A poster
- A newsletter to which all the different groups contribute.

These websites are excellent places to start your research for Activities 2 and 3: www.nutrition.org.uk/home.asp?siteId=43&sectionId=708&subSectionId=322&parentSection=299&which=1, the British Nutrition Foundation and www.food4life.org.uk/nutrient_sources

Case study 3 – Nutrition and teenagers

During adolescence iron requirements, increase to help with growth and muscle development. The National Diet and Nutrition Survey 2000 found 1 per cent of boys and 9 per cent of girls aged 15–18 had a haemoglobin level lower than recommended. Many teenage girls had a low intake of iron, with 50 per cent of 15–18 year olds having intakes below the lower reference nutrient intake (LRNI), implying that their intakes were likely to be inadequate. Those on poorly planned vegetarian diet or slimming may be particularly at risk. Bread flour is fortified with iron as are most breakfast cereals. Breakfast is an important way of acquiring iron. Although many adolescents do not eat breakfast, these foods can be encouraged as snacks instead, together with food or drink containing vitamin C, eg citrus fruit or a glass of fruit juice to enhance the absorption of iron.

The rapid increase in bone mass in teenagers means that they require more calcium than adults. Boys should aim for 1000 mg per day and girls 800 mg. Good sources of calcium include dairy products, including low fat versions (milk, yogurt and cheese). In the UK, white and brown flour must be fortified with calcium. Pulses, nuts, dried fruit and green vegetables, eg spring greens and broccoli, contain calcium. Fish that is eaten with the bones eg whitebait or canned sardines is also a good source. In some areas hard water provides a significant amount of calcium.

Amongst the findings of the 2000 survey were:

- The main sources of dietary energy for teenagers were cereal and cereal products, including bread, biscuits, buns, cakes and pastries, which together provided a third of dietary energy.

- Other sources of energy in the diet included vegetables, potatoes and savoury snacks which together contributed 15 per cent of energy in boys and 19 per cent in girls, and meat and meat products (which provided 15 per cent of energy in boys and 13 per cent in girls).

- Average intakes of saturated fats were higher than the adult recommendations (14 per cent vs 11 per cent of food energy).

- Some children had low intakes of some nutrients (see table below).

- Excluding salt added during cooking and at the table, daily sodium intakes were already higher than the RNI. This equates to 8.25 g of salt in boys aged 15–18 years and 5.75 g of salt in girls of the same age. Target salt intakes for sodium from all sources for people aged 15 plus are 6 g per day.

Teenagers need a varied diet, incorporating all the major food groups. In the short-term this will help with general appearance (eg shiny hair and healthy skin) and energy levels, while in the long term it will help prevent diseases such as cardiovascular disease and osteoporosis. (See table overleaf).

RNIs are used for protein, vitamins and minerals, and are an estimate of the amount that should meet the needs of most of the group to which they apply. They are not minimum targets. Intakes below the LRNI are almost certainly not enough for most people, so their diet is likely to be inadequate.

Source: www.nutrition.org.uk/home.asp?siteId=43&sectionId=397&subSectionId=315&
parentSection=299&which=1

Percentage of 15–18 year olds with intakes of nutrients below Lower Reference Nutritional Intake (LRNI)			Boys 15–18	Girls 15–18
Vitamin A	12	12		
Riboflavin	6	21		
Iron	2	50		
Calcium	9	19		
Zinc	9.9	10		
Magnesium	18	53		

INDIVIDUAL ACTIVITY

- Keep a food and drink (including fizzy drinks) diary for a week, listing what you eat, when and what quantities. Check the information of the packaging of foods to see what it contains, both for each of the main food groups and for vitamin and mineral content.
- If you drink alcohol, log this intake too!
- Compare your personal intake of nutrition to the recommended amounts. Are there any improvements you could make in your diet and nutrition?

Go to www.food4life.org.uk/adolescent/play_it/game. php?game=adolescent1 and check out your diet and nutrition knowledge!

ACTIVITY 3

Divide into groups and research why vitamin C, iron and calcium are so important in the diet of teenagers. Find out which foods contain these nutrients. Some other vital nutrients are listed in the table above. Add these to your research plus any other vitamins and minerals you come across in your research.

Also find out why too much sodium may be harmful, and how you can identify salt and sugar on the labels of packaged food and drinks (there are lots of different words used to describe ingredients that are basically sugars!).

- Produce a display (or PowerPoint presentation) summarising the need for these nutrients in your diet and the dangers of too much salt and sugar!

Case study 4 – Personal hygiene

One of the most effective ways we have to protect ourselves and others from illness is good personal hygiene. This means washing your hands, especially, but also your body. It means being careful not to cough or sneeze on others, cleaning things that you touch if you are unwell, putting items such as tissues (that may have germs) into a bin, and using protection (like gloves or condoms) when you might be at risk of catching an infection.

Body smells are caused by a number of factors working in combination, including:

- Chemicals in sweat, including pheromones, which are made by the body and sexually attract (or repel) other people
- Wastes excreted through the skin, such as metabolised alcohol
- The actions of bacteria that live on the skin and feed on dead skin cells and sweat
- Unwashed clothes, such as underwear and socks.

Most infections, especially colds and gastroenteritis, are caught when we put our unwashed hands, which have germs on them, to our mouth. Some infections are caught when other people's dirty hands touch the food we eat. Hands and wrists should be washed with clean soap and water, using a brush if your fingernails are dirty. Dry your hands with something clean, such as paper towels or hot-air dryers. You should always wash your hands:

- After using the toilet
- Before making or eating food
- After handling dogs or other animals
- If you have been around someone who is coughing or has a cold.

Good dental hygiene includes regular brushing. Bad breath can be caused by diseases of the teeth, gums and mouth, such as infections. Most people have bad breath first thing in the morning because saliva is not made while you're asleep. Some foods that can cause bad breath include garlic and onion. Mouthwashes and sprays can make your breath smell better for a while, but if you have a health problem in your mouth, you need to see your dentist.

*Source: www.betterhealth.vic.gov.au/bhcv2/bhcarticles.nsf/pages/Personal_*
hygiene?OpenDocument

ACTIVITY 4

Working in small groups, design a poster that highlights the importance of personal hygiene and explains why personal hygiene is important in the workplace.

Your posters could be displayed in class and also at the well-being day.

Case study 5 – Effects of alcohol on your health

Alcohol can affect a number of body systems, including:

- Cardiovascular system – raised blood pressure and triglycerides (especially after binge drinking), damage to the heart muscle and stroke
- Nervous system – brain damage, tremors, dementia and nerve damage. Alcohol is a depressant drug and affects your coordination, self-control, judgement and reaction times
- Gastrointestinal system – stomach inflammation (gastritis) and bleeding
- Liver – cancer, hepatitis (inflammation), fatty changes, cirrhosis and liver failure
- Endocrine system – problems controlling blood sugar, loss of libido and reduced fertility
- Nutrition – malnutrition (alcohol displaces nutrients from your body) and obesity.

Health benefits of alcohol:

- Very moderate amounts of alcohol may contain health benefits for older people by reducing the risk of some types of cardiovascular disease
- Research suggests the benefits are limited to men over the age of 40 who consume no more than two standard drinks daily, and women over the age of 50 who drink one standard drink daily or less
- These benefits do not extend to younger people. Alcohol may severely impair development in young people
- The risk of cirrhosis, some cancers and other diseases becomes greater with increased alcohol consumption.

Source: www.betterhealth.vic.gov.au/bhcv2/bhcarticles.nsf/pages/
Alcohol?OpenDocument

ACTIVITY 5

In groups, investigate the recommended safe daily maximums for alcohol. Find out what a 'unit' of alcohol is in terms of: wine (look at wines of different strengths or percentages of alcohol); spirits (look at different proofs or strengths); beers; fortified wines; alcopops.

Find out why it is potentially dangerous to exceed the recommended (both health-related and in terms of your own safety and that of others) allowances and also the dangers of 'binge' drinking where excessive amounts of alcohol are consumed in a short time.

- Produce a class newsletter or information leaflet aimed at your fellow students, highlighting the benefits of safe drinking and the issues around using alcohol irresponsibly.
- Copies of this leaflet could be available to hand out at your well-being event.

Useful sites to research are: http://owen.massey.net/alcopops/azlist.html/www.alcoholconcern.org.uk

INDIVIDUAL ACTIVITY

If you drink alcohol, compare your consumption from the log you kept earlier with the safe recommended consumption. How are you doing? Are you a responsible drinker? If not, now is the time to do something about your drinking habits.

Case study 6 – Ireland smoke ban cleans pub air

The smoking ban in Ireland has cut air pollution in pubs and improved bar-workers' health. The ban had led to an 83 per cent reduction in air pollution and an 80 per cent cut in cancer causing agents. A team from the Research Institute for a Tobacco Free Society in Dublin, studied environmental tobacco smoke exposure in 42 Dublin pubs and tested 73 bar workers who volunteered to take part in the study. The workers were all given lung function tests before the ban came in and again a year later. They were also asked about their workplace exposure to tobacco. They reported being exposed to tobacco for 40 hours per week before the ban came in, falling to 25 minutes afterwards – a 99 per cent decrease. Lung function tests improved and there were significant reductions in cough and phlegm production.

These results confirm that the approach of a total ban on smoking in the workplace is successful in reducing the exposure of workers to particles. An ASH spokesman said: 'Tobacco interests have continued to suggest that there is no evidence that other people's smoke is harmful. This study shows not only how direct the harm is but also shows how comprehensive smoke-free public places can reverse that harm.'

Source: http://news.bbc.co.uk/1/hi/health/6559215.stm/

Cigarette-buying age set to rise

The government is to raise the legal minimum age at which tobacco can be bought to 18 years. About 9 per cent of 11 to 15-year-olds smoke and ministers hope the move will reduce this figure. Smoking is dangerous at any age, but the younger people start, the more likely they are to become life-long smokers and to die early.

The government argues that raising the legal age to 18 will make it easier for retailers to spot under-age smokers. Ministers also believe that bringing the legal age for the purchase of tobacco into line with that of alcohol will reinforce the dangers of smoking to young people.

A recent survey suggested that only 23 per cent of children aged under 16 who tried to buy tobacco found it difficult to do so. Someone who starts smoking aged 15 is three times more likely to die of cancer due to smoking than someone who starts in their late 20s.

Source: http://news.bbc.co.uk/1/hi/health/6216523.stm/

ACTIVITY 6

1) In small groups, research the issues of smoking in the workplace and the impact of smoking on both the smoker and others who work or live with them.

   Find out what legislation exists in the UK and the rest of the EU regarding smoking at work.

   Does an employer have to provide smokers with a smoking area? Are smokers entitled to time off with pay for attending sessions to help them quit?

   Produce a fact sheet 'Everything you need to know about smoking, its effects and your rights at work'. Have this ready for the well-being event.

2) Hold a class debate on the proposition that 'Governments should not interfere with the right of individuals to smoke in public'.

Other useful websites to use for research

www.ash.org.uk/html/workplace/html/workplace.html
www.cancer.org/docroot/PED/content/PED_10_2X_Smoking_In_
The_Workplace.asp
www.workplacelaw.net/search.php?category_id=93
www.forestonline.org/output/Page1.as
www.acas.org.uk/index.aspx?articleid=16
www.bupa.co.uk/health_information

This site has information for employers about smoking, alcohol, drugs and stress:
www.businesslink.gov.uk/bdotg/action/detail?type=RESOURCES&it
emId=1074439079

National Drugs helpline:
http://talktofrank.com/home_html.aspx/
Independent Information on drugs:
www.drugscope.org.uk

Case study 7A – Drug use

All drugs (including alcohol and tobacco) affect the brain. Different drugs act on different areas and alter the chemical balance. These changes are responsible for the feelings and sensations associated with drug taking. Drugs may be more harmful for young people because their bodies and brains are still developing. Some drugs are more addictive than others. And some people are much more likely than others to become addicted.

Several drugs that are prescribed by doctors to treat medical conditions can be misused. Examples include tranquillisers (eg Valium) and painkillers (eg codeine, DF118). Ritalin, used to treat attention deficit hyperactivity disorder (ADHD), can also be misused. These drugs are prescribed in doses that meet the needs of individuals. It can be very dangerous if anyone else takes them. Taking alcohol with any prescription or over-the-counter drug (medicine) can also be very dangerous. Combining prescribed drugs and over-the-counter drugs with illegal drugs and alcohol is particularly risky.

In 2002, a national survey of school children was conducted in Scotland. This anonymous survey asked young people about drinking, smoking and their experience of drug use.

Drug group	Drug	Effects
Stimulants (Uppers)	Amphetamine Cocaine	Increase energy, activity, heart rate, blood pressure.
Depressants	Alcohol	Slow down reactions, heart rate, breathing.
(Downers)	Heroin Solvents	Decrease energy levels, slow down heart rate
Hallucinogens	Cannabis LSD Magic mushrooms	Cause hallucinations (see, hear and feel things differently).

The survey found:

- 34 per cent of 13 year olds said they had been offered a drug; 13 per cent said they had used a drug.
- 65 per cent of 15 year olds said they had been offered a drug; 37 per cent said they had used a drug.
- Cannabis was the most commonly used drug; 31 per cent of 15 year olds said they had taken it in the last year.
- Over half of 13 year olds said they have been drunk at least once.
- Use of drugs like heroin and cocaine was very rare in this age group (in fact, more 13 and 15 year olds said they had been offered, or had used, solvents).
- Girls and boys who smoked and drank alcohol regularly were more likely to take drugs.
- 13 and 15 year olds were less likely to take drugs than they were to drink alcohol and get drunk.

Case study 7B – Police Force to test officers for drugs – 22 April 2004

Warwickshire Police is believed to be the first force in the country to introduce random drug testing for its own officers. Between six and ten officers will be tested every month. In the past nine months, five officers have left the force over allegations of drug misuse.

Staff working in all areas of the force will be asked to give a urine sample for drug and alcohol testing on a random basis.

Officers will be offered help if they admit to drug or alcohol problems. The Deputy Chief Constable said he believed they were the first force in the country to go operational with this policy. 'If an officer is tested and it's found to be a serious drug misuse then we may consider a misconduct hearing but the first instance is to take a welfare approach. If an officer has a problem we would much rather they came forward and told us'.

A force spokesman said the safety and welfare of its officers was important as well as public confidence. The Warwickshire Police Federation said: 'If people come to the force and identify they have a drink or other substance problem the force occupational health department will help them through. But if they leave it to the eleventh hour and don't share it with anybody then the force now has a policy in place where disciplinary action will be taken or possibly criminal proceedings.'

Source: http://news.bbc.co.uk/1/hi/england/coventry_warwickshire/3650487.stm/

ACTIVITY 7

1) In small groups by agreement with your tutor, research one of the main drug groups listed in Case study 7A. Find out what effects taking these drugs can have, both in the short term and for long term users.

2) Produce and deliver a PowerPoint slide show which explains to the rest of the class the effects of the specific drug group. (You could also use this at the well-being day.)

3) Apart from health and fitness issues, why else might uniformed services be concerned about their staff misusing drugs and alcohol or becoming addicted?

What risks might be posed to both the individuals involved and to the uniformed service and its reputation? Look at Case study 7B.

In groups, write a fictitious newspaper article based on an imagined story of a police officer or paramedic caught dealing in drugs for their personal use.

ACTIVITY 8

Using Case studies 8A/8B as your starting point, research the issues surrounding stress at work and the cost of stress related illness.

Find out what employers' responsibilities are to manage stress in the workplace.

Working in small groups, produce a Frequently Asked Questions sheet explaining what stress at work is (including PTSD) and what employers should do to help employees suffering from stress.

Useful websites for research are:

www.acas.org.uk/index.aspx?articleid=700
www.hse.gov.uk/stress
www.dti.gov.uk/files/file25664.pdf
www.thompsons.law.co.uk/ltext/l0780001.htm

Case study 8A – How employers can help manage employee stress

Main causes of stress:

Demands: employees often become overloaded if they cannot cope with the amount of work or type of work they are asked to do

Control: employees can feel disaffected and perform poorly if they have no say over how and when they do their work

Support: levels of absence due to sickness often rise if employees feel they cannot talk to managers about issues that are troubling them

Relationships: a failure to build relationships based on good behaviour and trust can lead to problems related to discipline, grievances and bullying

Role: employees will feel anxious about their work and the organisation if they don't know what is expected of them

Change: change needs to be managed effectively or it can lead to uncertainty and insecurity

What employers can do about it:

- make sure employees understand what they have to do and how to do it
- meet training needs
- consider whether working flexible hours would help employees to manage demands

- involve employees in the way work is carried out
- consult employees about decisions
- build effective teams with responsibility for outcomes
- review performance to identify strengths and weaknesses

- give employees the opportunity to talk about issues causing stress
- be sympathetic and supportive
- keep employees informed about what is going on in the firm

- have clear procedures for handling misconduct and poor performance
- have clear procedures for employees to raise grievances
- tackle any instances of bullying and harassment and make it clear such behaviour will not be tolerated

- carry out a thorough induction for new employees using a checklist of what needs to be covered
- provide employees with a written statement of employment particulars
- give employees clear job descriptions
- maintain a close link between individual objectives and organisational goals

- plan ahead so changes can be signposted and managers and employees are prepared
- consult with employees about prospective changes so they have a real input and work together with you to solve problems

Source: www.acas.org.uk/index.aspx?articleid=815

Other useful source of information: www.hse.gov.uk/stress/standards/index.htm

109

Case study 8B – Post-traumatic stress

Soldiers suffering psychological traumas years after serving in a war also experience poorer physical health, a series of studies suggest. Those with post-traumatic stress disorder were more likely to develop heart disease and cancer in later life than fellow war veterans.

The reasons are unclear but may be down to stress hormone levels, experts say. New Scientist pieced together evidence including surveys of more than 18 000 who had served in the Vietnam war. The research team at the New York Academy of Medicine divided the 18 000 veterans into those who suffered from post-traumatic stress disorder (PTSD) and those who did not. Those with PTSD were far more likely to die from accidents, drugs or suicide. Those who developed PTSD as a result of the stresses of war were also more likely to die of heart disease and various types of cancer.

A recent report showed Israeli veterans with PTSD after the combat in Lebanon in 1982 were twice as likely to have high blood pressure, ulcers and diabetes and five times as likely to have heart disease and headaches as those who did not develop PTSD. Research suggests anxiety and depression can have a negative effect on the body, such as making the heart more vulnerable to irregular heart beats and increase the risk of blood clotting. Stressed war veterans may also be more likely to lead unhealthy lifestyles, smoking and drinking excess alcohol, which could in turn lead to poorer physical health.

Sources: http://news.bbc.co.uk/1/hi/health/4179602.stm

www.newscientist.com/channel/health/mental-health/
mg18725143.800-trauma-of-war-hits-troops-years-later.html

NHS to assess post-bombs stress

People affected by the London suicide bombings are to be assessed for post traumatic stress. An NHS screening service is being offered to those who were injured or bereaved in the attacks. It will also be available to emergency workers and those who witnessed the 7 July bombings, which killed 52 people and injured 700, or their aftermath. Those showing trauma symptoms could be offered specialist treatment, to help them cope. Experts estimate around one in four people directly involved in the bombings may benefit from treatment for traumatic stress. The main symptoms of post traumatic stress disorder include flashbacks, sleeping problems, anxiety and irritability. They are common in the immediate aftermath of a traumatic event, but can be problematic if they emerge or continue to persist weeks later. It is normal to experience distress after involvement in a traumatic incident such as the London bombings. Most people will be coming to terms with the events of July, with the help of their family and friends. It is only several weeks after the traumatic incident however, if symptoms of distress don't naturally ease, that you can determine whether someone might benefit from specialist trauma support.

The NHS and emergency services responded magnificently to the London bombings on 7 July, and now the capital's mental health services are responding quickly and effectively to meet the long-term needs of victims and witnesses.

Source: http://news.bbc.co.uk/1/hi/health/4197536.stm

INDIVIDUAL ACTIVITY

Stress management – quiz

1) You're in the '10 items or less' express lane at the supermarket and you notice someone ahead of you has over 12 items in their basket. You:

   A Call for the manager

   B Don't let it bother you

   C Complain under your breath to the person behind you.

2) You know exactly which situations make you feel stressed:

   A Always

   B Never

   C Sometimes.

3) The amount of stress you experience in a difficult situation is influenced by:

   A Your thoughts and feelings

   B Your behaviour

   C All of the above.

4) You prepare yourself for stressful situations in advance by rehearsing how you will handle them:

   A Always

   B Never

   C Sometimes.

5) Your average day always includes time for exercise and fun:

   A Never – you don't have the time

   B Always

   C Only at weekends.

6) Your boss tells you off. You are upset and you:

   A Tell yourself you probably deserved it

   B Yell back

   C Wait till you both calm down then talk to the boss about it.

7) You were planning a weekend away with a friend who rings you at the last minute to cancel. You:

   A Hang up in a rage

   B Try and organise someone else to go with you

   C Go out with your mates.

8) When things go wrong you tend to think:

   A 'This is a disaster – I can't cope'

   B 'This is a challenge I can meet'

   C 'I'm out of here!'

Source: www.betterhealth.vic.gov.au

INDIVIDUAL ACTIVITY

National data suggests that a majority of teenagers in Britain are largely inactive, with 46 per cent of boys and 69 per cent of girls aged 15–18 spending less than one hour a day participating in activities of moderate intensity. The 2004 report At Least Five a Week, Evidence on the impact of physical activity and its relationship to health from the Chief Medical Officer recommended that teenagers (and children) have at least 60 minutes of at least moderate intensity exercise every day. It also recommended that activities that increase muscle strength and flexibility and also improve bone strength should be included at least twice a week.

Source: www.nutrition.org.uk/home.asp?siteId=43&sectionId=397&subSectionId=315& parentSection=299&which=1

Keep a log of all your physical activity for at least a week. The table on the next page could be used as a format for recording this.

- At the end of the week analyse your log against the requirements of the recommendation for teenagers to exercise at least five times a week, ideally for 60 minutes every day, to at least moderate levels of intensity.
- If you are not meeting these targets you should be setting yourself an action plan and taking every opportunity provided both through school/college and in your social activities to increase your participation in exercise.
- Could you walk briskly to school/college rather than getting the bus? What other simple steps could you take? Could you go to the gym or play sport at lunchtime?
- For a career in a uniformed public service you will need to be physically fit, not only for the entry test but to carry out your role effectively all throughout your career, so you need to get started now!
- Evaluate your log against the following criteria:
  - **a)** progression
  - **b)** your attitude
  - **c)** your motivation
  - **d)** achievement of goals.

Day	Activity	Duration/time	Intensity (H/M/L)
Monday			
Tuesday			
Wednesday			
Thursday			
Friday			
Saturday			
Sunday			

Evaluation of my week's exercise log

Progress Did I get better as the week went on? If not, why?			
Attitude How positive was I to my exercise schedule?			
Motivation Which activity motivates me most? Why?			
Goals How close am I do achieving my goal of entry to my chosen uniformed service?			

Case study 9

When designing a fitness programme, various principles should be taken into account. A common one used by fitness specialists is FITT – frequency, intensity, time, type.

	Term	Meaning	Standard recommendation
F	Frequency	How often you exercise	5–6 times per week
I	Intensity	How hard you exercise	Moderate to high
T	Time	How long you exercise for	Anywhere from 15–40 minutes
T	Type	The kind of exercise you undertake	Most exercise, from brisk walking to high intensity sports

All fitness-training programmes contain the elements of **frequency** and **intensity**. Training frequency refers to the number of training sessions performed. Whereas training intensity is the effort required to perform an exercise. It is usually referred to as a percentage of maximum and common tools used to measure intensity are heart rate monitors and scales of perceived exertion.

The **time** you spend exercising is also important. The time dedicated to exercise usually depends on the type of exercise undertaken. For example, it is recommended that to improve cardiovascular fitness you will need at least 20 to 30 minutes of non-stop exercise. For weight loss at least 40 minutes of moderate weight bearing exercise is required. However, when talking about the time required for muscular strength improvements, time is often measured as a number of 'sets' and 'reps'. A typical recommendation would be 3 sets of 8 repetitions.

Like time, the **type** of exercise you choose will have a big effect on the results you achieve. That is why it is important to know what you want to gain from your efforts. If you hope to improve your cardiovascular fitness, then exercises like walking, jogging, swimming, bike riding, stair climbing, aerobics and rowing are all effective.

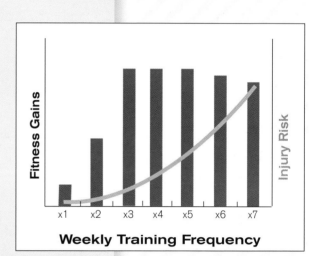

Improvements with **fitness** will occur with an increase in weekly training **frequency**. Research has demonstrated that a frequency of 3 to 5 training sessions per week will improve cardiovascular fitness levels. However, the magnitude of the change becomes increasingly smaller and tends to plateau after a frequency of 3 sessions per week. The risk of injury increases disproportionately if training is performed too frequently due to the excessive strain applied to the joints, muscles etc. When considering which of the two elements, **frequency** or **intensity**, have the greatest effect upon fitness levels, it is the **intensity** at which exercise is performed that counts, although a structured training programme should allow for both. In terms of percentage gains per minute of training performed, training intensity has the greatest impact. That's more improvement in less training time! If training frequency needs to be decreased, then simply increase the intensity of your remaining sessions.

High intensity training can also be associated with an increased risk of over-training, a decrease in physical performance despite continued training, as high intensity takes more out of the body and takes longer to recover from. High intensity training requires a decent level of initial fitness in order to perform effectively.

The principle of specificity plays a major role in the changes to fitness levels that occur following exercise training, as adaptations are highly specific to the nature of the training performed.

http://mysite.wanadoo-members.co.uk/corshamref/sub/fitness/fitpasstest.htm/

ACTIVITY 9

When designing your own fitness training programme you need to consider your chosen uniformed public service and both the entry and ongoing fitness requirements (for example, to join the prison service you have to pass the entry test, but in your role as an officer you need to maintain your fitness for Control and Restraint activities as part of your duties on a Wing).

114

In groups, research the following concepts to assist you with designing your training programme and produce an information leaflet to summarise your findings (for the rest of the class and for the well-being event).

Principles of training:

- www.bbc.co.uk/schools/gcsebitesize/pe/training/trainingrev2.shtml
- www.bbc.co.uk/schools/gcsebitesize/pe/training/trainingrev3.shtml
- www.bbc.co.uk/schools/gcsebitesize/pe/training/trainingrev4.shtml
- www.bbc.co.uk/schools/gcsebitesize/pe/training/trainingrev5.shtml
- www.bbc.co.uk/schools/gcsebitesize/pe/training/trainingrev6.shtml eg individual needs

Periodisation:

- Macrocycle
- Mesocycle
- Microcycle.

Training techniques:

- Resistance training
- Continuous training
- Interval training
- Circuit training.

www.bbc.co.uk/schools/gcsebitesize/pe/training/trainingrev1.shtml
www.brianmac.demon.co.uk/trnprin.htm
www.pponline.co.uk/encyc/periodisation.html
www.runnersweb.com
www.trainingsmartonline.com/images/Free_Triathlon_Articles/Periodisation.pdf
www.coachingireland.com/article/article_9.shtml
www.itftennis.com/shared/medialibrary/pdf/original/IO_8623_original.PDF

This site has an online quiz you could try!
www.teachpe.com/cloze/principles_training.htm

INDIVIDUAL ACTIVITY – THE EXERCISE SAFELY QUIZ

1) What is the first symptom of dehydration?

    A Headache.

    B Fatigue.

    C Thirst.

2) How much fluid does the average athlete lose during each hour of exercise?

    A One litre.

    B One and a half litres.

    C Half a litre.

115

3) What is the best way to prevent dehydration when playing sport or exercising?

A Drink water before, during and after exercising.

B Listen to your body and drink only when you feel thirsty.

C Drink as much water as you can after exercising.

4) Running, jogging or even walking on hard surfaces can cause injuries to joints, bones and muscles. What is the most important thing you can do to reduce the risk of injury?

A Run barefoot.

B Wear appropriate running shoes to cushion the impact.

C Choose soft, level surfaces such as a running track, grassy oval or the beach.

5) How many recovery days should you have during any given week?

A One.

B None.

C Two.

6) How important is well-maintained equipment in preventing injuries?

A Not at all – good technique is everything.

B Reasonably important.

C Vital – poorly maintained equipment is a common cause of injury.

7) What's the best way to treat a soft tissue injury, such as a sprain?

A Ice the injured area for 20 minutes every two hours for 48 hours, and rest until you feel better.

B Work through the injury, since a good blood supply can speed along the healing process.

C Apply an ice pack to the injured part immediately following the injury, and rest the following day.

Case study 10 – Fitness required of uniformed services personnel

Explosive strength plays a key role in the successful completion of many crucial fire service tasks. Maximal efforts are frequently required to perform urgent duties such as: forcing doors, moving heavy objects, and evacuating injured people.

Muscular endurance is also of vital importance, for nearly every fire rescue and suppression-related task requires numerous, not just one, two, or three repetitions. For instance, the operation of a nozzle, ascending stairs, and victim transport all require either continuous muscle use for extended duration or repetitious muscle contraction.

To improve strength – To improve your explosive power, you should exercise with relatively high weights and complete very few repetitions (1–5). To improve your muscular endurance, you need to complete a higher numbers of repetitions with lower weights.

25–30 repetitions at a weight that causes you to tire, but, still maintain good form is quite productive.

Source: www.nyc.gov/html/fdny/html/fitness/fitness_strength.shtm

Bedfordshire Police entry tests

The job related fitness test is designed to assess those areas of fitness required to cope with the nature and extent of physical demands placed upon street duty policing.

Dynamic strength

This test involves performing five seated chest presses and five seated back pulls, on a piece of equipment called a Dyno Strength test machine. The average force of the sum of the five presses, and the average force of the sum of the five pulls will be recorded. The lowest score recorded will determine the overall level awarded.

Preparation – The best way to practise or improve the level attained in this element is to work and develop your upper body muscles. A body weight exercise that would work the muscles, which is responsible for pressing and pulling, would be press-ups. Make sure you do a full range of motion on each press up going all the way down to the floor and fully locking out the elbows. Keep your body straight and use a mirror or get someone to watch you. Aim to practise for 10 to 15 minutes 3 to 4 times a week. Perform the press ups at a rate of approximately 25 per minute. Do as many as possible and then rest for 90 seconds. Do this another three times, making sure you are fully locking the elbows and keeping your back straight.

Endurance

During this element you run to and fro along a 15 metre track in time to a series of audible beeps. The pace becomes progressively faster as the test continues. You must run for as long as possible until you can no longer keep up with the required speed. This test is very similar to a 'Shuttle Run' or 'Bleep Test' which you may have experienced elsewhere.

Preparation – To prepare for this test it is recommended that you do continuous jogging for 20–30 minutes without a break. You should practise three to four times a week.

Source: www.bedfordshire.police.uk/?–id=442

You can download a copy of the South Yorkshire Police bleep test from:
www.southyorks.police.uk/careers/regulars/fitnesstest.php

West Midlands Police test
www.west-midlands.police.uk/wmprrecruit/
wmpr2006130133436.asp

INDIVIDUAL ACTIVITY

Research the entry fitness requirements for your chosen uniformed service. Analyse those in terms of: aerobic capacity; strength; muscular endurance; flexibility.

Identify what types of training will help you to improve your fitness for these entry tests and use that information to help you when designing your personal fitness plan.

Case study 11 – Sit-up test

Abdominal muscle strength and endurance is important for core stability and back support. This sit-up test measures the strength and endurance of the abdominals and hip-flexor muscles. How many sit-ups can you do in one minute? Keep a record and see if you can increase the number.

Starting position: Lie on a carpeted or cushioned floor with your knees bent at approximately right angles, with feet flat on the ground. Your hands should be resting on your thighs.

Technique: Squeeze your stomach, push your back flat and raise high enough for your hands to slide along your thighs to touch the tops of your knees. Don't pull with you neck or head and keep your lower back on the floor. Then return to the starting position.

INDIVIDUAL ACTIVITY – ANSWERS

How well did you do? Do you need to work on this?

Scoring for stress management quiz activity

Question		Scores	
	A	**B**	**C**
1	1	10	6
2	10	1	6
3	1	6	10
4	10	1	6
5	1	10	6
6	6	1	10
7	1	10	6
8	1	10	6

What your score means

Score 0 to 20: You tend to bottle things up until you reach exploding point. Try talking about your worries before they get too big to handle. Make more time in your life for relaxation and develop some strategies to let off steam constructively.

Score 21 to 59: You talk about what's stressing you out but often not to the person who can most help. Try rehearsing situations that are stressful for you and imagine yourself handling them more confidently. Avoiding situations that you find stressful only works to a point. Take on achievable projects at home or at work that will build your sense of confidence and achievement and develop your problem-solving and goal-setting skills.

Score 60 to 80: You are a good stress manager. You know what your stress triggers are and you are able to handle them when they arise.

Answers to exercise safety activity

Question	1	2	3	4	5	6	7
Correct response	B	B	A	C	C	C	A

Score 0 to 2: You're probably on first-name terms with the staff at your local emergency department. It's in your best interests to find out more about exercise safety by talking to your coach, sports trainer, physiotherapist or registered fitness instructor.

Score 3 to 5: You have a basic understanding of exercise safety, but the gaps in your knowledge could injure you. Reduce your risk by brushing up on your incorrect answers.

Score 6 to 7: You show a good general knowledge of exercise safety issues.

See your tutor for further suggestions on how to reduce your risk of sports-related injuries!

MARKED ASSIGNMENTS

Unit 1 – Government, Policies and the Public Services

SAMPLE ASSIGNMENT

How government develops policy and manages uniformed public services.

BACKGROUND INFORMATION

The UK government is responsible for developing policyies and passing legislation through Parliament. Policies have to gain parliamentary and public support and must be implemented.

UK Government departments have a large number of functions for which they are responsible, which may change over time as different administrations try to streamline public administration and as changes in the national and international context occur.

The split of Home Office functions in May 2007 and the establishment of the Ministry of Justice was justified in part by the terrorism in the USA (9/11) and the London Bombings in July 2005.

Included in the functions and responsibilities of central government departments are the overseeing of the direction and values of the UK uniformed public services.

Some uniformed public services, such as the ambulance services, the police and the fire and rescue services, also have accountabilities to their relevant statutory authorities and to their local authority (and thus to the local community).

In addition, the UK uniformed public services have to be held responsible to various statutory inspectorates and other bodies, such as the Prison Service Independent Monitoring Boards, and their performance is measured in the public documents they publish, such as annual reports, objectives, mission statements, internal complaints and procedures, management procedures.

This assignment will enable you to show that you can:

> *P4 explain the development process of government policies*
>
> *M3 analyse the development process of government policies*
>
> *P3 describe three government departments and their responsibility for specific uniformed public services.*

Remember that you must list your reference sources at the end of your work in a bibliography. This list should include the titles of websites and newspapers or magazines you have used, the titles and authors of textbooks you have referred to, and information on any other uniformed public services booklets or documents you have quoted from or used for reference.

Task 1 P4, M3

Write an essay which **explains how UK government policies are developed** (P4) **and analyses this development process** (M3).

You will need to include details of development processes from when legislation is first conceived through to the point at which it becomes an Act of Parliament and is implemented. Try to use real examples to illustrate the processes.

The checklist below is based on the content of Unit 1:

Creating policy
    Role of Cabinet
    White Papers and Green Papers
    Consultation and representations
    Drafting of the statute
    Laying before Parliament
    Parliamentary readings
    Voting in Parliament
    Royal assent
    Implementation.

Task 2 P3

Select **three government departments** to investigate.

Research these departments and their specific responsibilities for named uniformed public services.

Produce and deliver a PowerPoint presentation which **describes three government departments and their responsibilities** for specific uniformed public services.

MERIT LEVEL ANSWER

Task 1
How government policies are developed, by Paul Green, BTEC National Public Services

UK Government policy is developed in a number of ways depending on whether it is policy due to political commitment (like the Human Rights Act 1998, which was part of the Labour Party Manifesto at the previous election) or due to public pressure (like the proposal in March 2007 to legislate on Climate Change) or as a result of international agreements such as an EU Directive (example is age discrimination).

Once a policy has been thought of it is discussed, usually in Cabinet, although if it was as a result of EU Directives, like Age Discrimination law, it may be discussed through consultation papers with the public or all parties in Parliament.

To consult further the government may issue a Green Paper, which is an open consultation or a White Paper (which means government have decided to do something but are consulting on HOW to do it).

Green and White papers and draft Bills are all open for public consultation, often for a designated period of time. Also lobby groups and pressure groups try to influence government and their policy making processes.

The Bill does not take shape in isolation. Ministers and civil servants carry out extensive informal consultations to ensure that it covers everything and works in practice. The people and organisations consulted vary according to the subject matter of the Bill. They generally include experts, trade organisations, unions, MPs and other politicians, the Treasury and other government departments and international agencies.

A controversial Bill may go to the Cabinet, or to one of its Committees, for further discussion. Bills are increasingly being published in draft form to allow more time for public discussion and consultation. When the Bill has been drafted, agreed by Ministers, and consulted upon, it is ready to be laid before parliament. Bills can start in either the House of Commons (most usual) or the House of Lords. It is for Government Ministers to decide. This is also known as 'the first reading'.

There are also some Bills put before parliament that are not government ones – Private Members Bills are put to parliament in each session. They have only a small chance of becoming law.

MPs take part in a ballot and the successful MPs get parliamentary time to introduce their Bills.

A third type of legislation is Private Bills before Parliament.

You could have developed this a bit more.
Good examples which could have been explained in more depth.

Good – you understand the differences.

Good summary which gives an overview of the potential scope of such consultation!

Useful to include – examples?

123

Private Bills are bills which are promoted by organisations outside the House (eg local authorities or companies) to obtain powers for themselves in excess of, or in conflict with, the general law.

The second reading debate is a general and wide-ranging debate about the Bill. It usually lasts for a day – more complex and controversial measures will be discussed for longer.

If the Bill is at all controversial, the debate ends with a vote. It is very rare for a Government Bill to be defeated at second reading as the government has a majority of MPs.

The Bill then goes to Committee stage where it is examined in detail by a committee of 18 to 25 MPs representing the different political parties. The Bill then passes on to the Report stage where any amendments made by Committee are considered. The Bill then goes back to the House of Commons for the third reading.

After its third reading the Bill automatically moves on to The House of Lords. It goes through similar processes but the Committee stage in the Lords is on the floor of the House so all Peers can join in the discussions. If a Bill passes through the House of Lords unchanged, it is immediately sent for Royal Assent. If any amendments have been made, the Bill returns to the Commons to debate the Lords amendments. The Commons can accept the amendments in which case that is the end of the matter or it can replace them or reject them. If so the Bill returns to the Lords again with a statement of 'reasons' for the Commons action. The Lords generally accepts the situation because the Commons are elected representatives (MPs) and the Lords are unelected. The Lords cannot delay Bills for more than one parliament and Finance Bills (and taxation) are not discussed by the Lords.

On 28 March 2007 Peers inflicted a defeat on the government rejecting plans for a super casino in Manchester and 16 other casinos. In a surprise vote the Lords rejected the government's regulations by 123 to 120. It was only the third time in the last 50 years that the Lords rejected secondary legislation. They backed an amendment declining to approve the Gambling Order and calling for a joint committee of the Lords and the Commons to look again at the decision-making process.

(The primary legislation was the Gaming Act 2006 which was passed by both Houses of Parliament, the secondary legislation was the Order needed to implement part of the Gaming Act 2006)

When a Bill has passed through all its parliamentary stages, it is sent to the monarch for Royal Assent, after which it becomes an Act of Parliament. The Royal Assent has not been refused since 1707.

124

Tutor feedback

Examples?

How does parliament organise the vote or Division?

Good understanding or roles of both chambers.

Excellent illustration!

Good – you have made the distinction between primary and secondary.

What do you conclude from this about the power of the monarch?

When an Act comes into force depends on its wording. In some cases, its provisions apply immediately. In others, a starting-date (or more than one if different parts of an Act may come into force at different times) is laid down in the Act. In other cases, a Commencement Order must be made to activate the Act, or certain parts of it. These delays in implementation give government departments and other interest groups time to prepare for the changes the Act will bring about.

Once the Act has been implemented it is the law of the land. The lengthy and thorough process of legislation has finally come to its conclusion.

For example, the Freedom of Information Act 2000 didn't come into force until 1 January 2005. It gave rights to access information held by 100,000 public bodies, including individual schools and GP surgeries. To allow everyone to prepare for this over four years from royal assent to implementation were allowed. During that time codes of practice were drawn up and adverts and publicity made the public aware of their new rights. All public bodies had to review their processes so they were able to comply with the new requirements. Staff had to be trained in how to deal with requests under the Act.

Why is the process so complex? There are a number of reasons, but they really all come down to the UK being a democracy. Lots of the legislation that is passed is not party political or controversial but even things that appear straightforward, like equality legislation can create debate, sometimes when the legislation is being passed through parliament and at other times, like the super casino legislation, when the legislation is being implemented.

Another recent controversy was to do with the implementation of The Equality Act (2006) which covered the creation of the Commission on Equality and Human Rights (CEHR), the outlawing of discrimination of provision of goods and services on the grounds of religion and belief and allowed government to introduce regulations outlawing discrimination on the ground of sexual orientation in provision of goods and services (the Sexual Orientation Regulations 2006). The government announced in January 2007 that no exemption would be made for Catholic and other faith based adoption agencies in the implementation of these Regulations but they would be given a transition period until the end of 2008 to adapt to the new rules which, having been delayed for 6 months, were due to commence in April 2007.

Having open and honest debate at all stages of the process from legislation being conceived to it becoming law and being implemented means that, while not everyone will agree with everything, at least different points of view can be heard and the lobbying by those in parliament and

An excellent example to use because this legislation had such wide ranging impact on so many public bodies.

Good analysis.

Excellent analysis and a good example to select as there are two interesting conflicts of rights here – non discrimination and religious beliefs!

government, the general public and interest and faith groups should result in legislation that is seen as honest and open and that most people can sign up to – in other words, legislation that will work and be enforced.

The system in the UK is open and public. Draft legislation and policy development is available on the many government web sites and comment is actively invited from individuals, groups and companies.

Parliamentary proceedings are openly reported in the press and media and are recorded word for word in *Hansard* (which can be accessed online at http://www.publications.parliament.uk/pa/cm/cmhansrd.htm).

Since 1907 The Department of the Official Report – also known as *Hansard* – has been responsible for producing reports of the proceedings of the main Chamber of the House of Commons, of Westminster Hall and of Standing Committees. These have been published and so 100 years of records are available!

Task 2 – Government Departments – a slide show which describes 3 government departments and their responsibilities for specific uniformed public services by Paul Green ace presenter.

Web sites used for my research
http://www.pm.gov.uk/ http://www.direct.gov.uk/ http://www.parliamentary-counsel.gov.uk/
http://www.parliament.uk/
http://www.communities.gov.uk/

Good justification for UK parliamentary system and processes!

Important in a democracy!

See comments on feedback sheet.

Did you use any other sites?

Task 2 – Government Departments

Slide one

Task 2 – Government Departments

A slide show which describes 3 government departments and their responsibilities for specific uniformed public services

by Paul Green ace presenter

Slide two

Government Departments

The government departments which have specific responsibilities for uniformed public services are:-

Home Office
Ministry of Justice
Ministry of Defence
Dept of Communities
& Local Government
(DCLG)

Department of Health
HM Revenue and
Customs
Dept of Transport

Can you guess which uniformed public service belongs where?

Slide three

1. Ministry of Defence	a. Prisons
2. Ministry of Justice	b. Army, Navy, RAF
3. Home Office	c. Fire & Rescue Services
4. HMRC	d. HM Customs
5. Dept of Health	e. Ambulance Services
6. Dept of Transport	f. Police
7. DCLG	g. Immigration Services
8. Treasury	h. Coastguard

Slide four

The Answers

1. Ministry of Defence – Armed Forces **b**.
2. Ministry of Justice – Prisons **a**.
3. Home Office – Police & Immigration **f**. **g**.
4. HMRC – Customs **d**.
5. Dept of Health – Ambulance **e**.
6. Dept of Transport – Coastguard **h**.
7. DCLG – Fire & Rescue **c**.
8. Treasury – **all of them** as it sets the budgets!

How many did you get right??

Slide five

The 3 departments I am going to describe are:-

- Ministry of Justice
- Department of Health
- Ministry of Defence

Slide six

Ministry of Justice

This Department came into being in May 2007 and is responsible for criminal, civil, family and administrative justice system, the courts, tribunals, legal aid, prison and Probation.

It is headed by the Secretary of State for Justice.

Slide seven

Ministry of Justice

Both HM Prisons and Private Prisons come under this Ministry as does probation. The overall section managing prisons and probation is NOMs

(National Offender Management Service).

Slide eight

Ministry of Justice

The budget for the prison service comes from the Ministry of Justice (agreed with Treasury) and the Director General of HMPS is accountable for the use of the budget and the performance of the prisons. The Ministry of Justice sets the performance standards and targets that the prison service has to work to on an annual basis. The Secretary of State for Justice decides on things like the building of new prisons or the use of Police cells to house offenders.

Slide nine

Managing the Prisons

Other independent bodies that help in managing the prisons are

- HM Inspector Of Prisons
- Prison and Probation Ombudsman
- The Independent Monitoring Boards
- Audit Office (all part of the public sector are subject to audit of their work & finances)

Slide ten

The Independent Monitoring Boards

Inside every prison and immigration removal centre there is an IMB

Members are independent and unpaid, appointed by Government Ministers to monitor the day-to-day life in their local prison or removal centre and ensure that proper standards of care and decency are maintained.

Slide eleven

The Prisons and Probation Ombudsman

- Is appointed by the government to investigate complaints from prisoners and those subject to probation supervision
- Is completely independent of both the Prison Service and the National Probation Service (NPS)
- Is also responsible for investigating all deaths of prisoners and in probation hostels and immigration detention accommodation.

Slide twelve

HM Inspector Of Prisons

- an independent inspectorate which reports on conditions for and treatment of those in prison, young offender institutions and immigration removal centres
- reports are public published documents
- is paid for by the government

Slide thirteen

Department of Health

- has overall responsibility for all NHS Trusts including the 13 NHS Ambulance Trusts
- headed by a Secretary of State who is a cabinet minister and elected MP
- sets overall performance targets for the ambulance Trusts and monitors their achievement of these targets

Each NHS Ambulance Trust is managed by a locally appointed Chief Executive and a Board.

Slide fourteen

NHS Ambulance Trusts

- Currently there are 13 regional trusts
- They are overseen by an NHS Board headed by a Chairman
- On a day to day basis they are managed by a CEO
- They have targets set by the DoH
- They produce strategic plans and annual reports
- They have to publish performance achievements
- The Healthcare Commission inspects their quality and value for money

Slide fifteen

Ministry of Defence

- Headed by a secretary of state for defence with other government ministers
- Responsible for all armed forces, regular and reserves
- Undertakes defence planning, arms control, intelligence and security

Slide sixteen

MoD

- provides the defence capabilities to ensure the security and defence of the UK & Overseas Territories
- supports the government's foreign policy especially peace & security.
- responsibility for Armed Forces; 200,000 regular members of Army, Royal Navy & RAF; 47,000 reserves
- leads government policy of defence diplomacy through NATO, EU, UN
- provides UK strategic direction in conflict prevention, crisis management and operations

Slide seventeen

MoD

- procures equipment which is cost effective & meets military needs through the Defence Procurement Agency (fighter aircraft, tanks, submarines)
- supports UK defence exports
- funds the Meteorological Office (provides national weather forecasts)
- operates military schools and academies, including Sandhurst
- provides services for military veterans, including war pensions

Slide eighteen

Armed Forces

- The highest military post within the MOD is the Chief of the Defence Staff. This job is filled by a senior officer from one of the three Services. CDS is the professional head of the Armed Forces and is the principal military advisor to the Secretary of State.
- The top Civil Servant in the MoD is known as the Permanent Secretary with responsibility for finance, planning and administration of the MOD

Slide nineteen

Armed Forces

Each of the three Services has a permanent Chief of Staff at the MoD

eg Chief of the Air Staff (CAS) has the rank of Air Chief Marshal.

CAS is the senior advisor to the Chief of Defence Staff on air power

Slide twenty

And finally

Other parts of government with responsibilities for uniformed public services

Slide twenty one

The Police

- **Home Office** set strategic direction
- **Local Police Authority** and **Chief Constable** manage on day to day basis
- In London, **Greater London Authority** and **Met Police Authority** liaise together
- Elsewhere **local councils** liaise with police authorities
- The **Independent Police Complaints Commission** (IPCC) investigates complaints
- **Her Majesty's Inspectors of Constabulary** inspects performance

Slide twenty two

Fire & Rescue Services

- Dept Communities and local government set targets & direction
- Managed on day to day basis by Independent local Fire Authority and Chief Officer
- Liaise closely with local government
- In London report to Greater London Authority and London Mayor
- Chief Fire and Rescue Adviser's Unit inspects performance and helps share good practice

ASSESSOR FEEDBACK FORM

BTEC National Uniformed Public Service
Unit 1 Government, Policies and the Uniformed Public Services
Paul Green, BTEC National Year 1 Public Services

Task 1 (P4, M3), Task 2 (P3)

Tutor feedback

Task 1

Paul, this is an excellent explanation of the development of government policy. You have included all relevant stages and have analysed the process and illustrated it with recent relevant examples.

Task 2

Your PowerPoint slideshow is well thought out and includes all required information. You have outlined well the way the different levels of government are involved with the uniformed public services and which part of government (central, regional, local) has what responsibility and how the various inspectorates monitor the performance of the specific uniformed services you have discussed.

Your presentation was excellent – the use of the quiz got everyone's interest right at the beginning of your talk and is a good technique to use! Well done.

Grading criteria achieved: P3, P4, M3

Assessor Observation Record	
Learner's name:	Paul Green
Programme:	BTEC National Year 1 Public Services
Unit number & title:	Unit 1 Government, Policies and the Uniformed Public Services

Activity observed – presentation on government departments and uniformed public services

TASK 2 P3
Select three government departments to investigate. Research these departments and their specific responsibilities for named uniformed public services.
Produce and deliver a PowerPoint presentation which **describes** three government departments and their responsibilities for specific uniformed public services.

How the activity meets the requirements of the learning outcomes and grading criteria

Your presentation was excellent – the use of the quiz got everyone's interest right at the beginning of your talk and is a good technique to use! Well done.
When presenting your slideshow you added further explanation to each of the slides showing that you clearly understood the complexities of the relationships between central government departments, local accountabilities, inspectorates and the accountabilities uniformed public services have to the general public which they serve.
Your PowerPoint slideshow was well thought out and included all required information. You have outlined well the way the different levels of government are involved with the uniformed public services, which part of government (central, regional, local) has what responsibility, and how the various inspectorates monitor the performance of the specific services you have discussed.

Candidate	Paul Green	**Assessor**	J Chapmann
Date	15 May 2007		

UNIT 2 – Team Leadership in the Uniformed Public Services

SAMPLE ASSIGNMENT

Practical demonstration of leadership skills.

BACKGROUND INFORMATION

The ability to lead teams is vital for a career in the uniformed public services. In previous assignments you have looked at leadership styles, the role of the leader and the skills and qualities required to lead teams effectively.

You have looked at barriers to good team-work and how to overcome them, and the communication skills required when briefing and debriefing the team.

In this assignment you will put theory into practice, ensuring that the teams you lead achieve the required objectives. You will need to demonstrate that you have the skills to deal effectively with team members, encouraging and supporting them, motivating and dealing with potential conflict.

You will also be expected to understand methods to evaluate effective team leadership and use those methods to evaluate your own performance as a leader and draw up a development plan for improving your own skills.

This assignment will enable you to show that you can:

> *P6 describe different types of teams and the stages of team development*
>
> *P5 describe evaluation methods used to assess effective team leadership*
>
> *P4 use appropriate skills to lead a team in the practical implementation of a plan*
>
> *M3 demonstrate effective leadership skills when leading a team in the practical implementation of a plan to achieve a given task*

> *D2 evaluate your own ability to provide effective team leadership, making recommendations for your own development and improvement.*

Remember that you must list your reference sources at the end of your work in a bibliography. This list should include the titles of websites and newspapers or magazines you have used, the titles and authors of textbooks you have referred to, and information on any other uniformed public services booklets or documents you have quoted from or used for reference.

Logging and evaluating your leadership experiences

At the start of the year you were briefed by your tutor to log any opportunities you had to take part in team activities (for Unit 4) or to lead a team in achieving a task (Unit 2).

You were also asked to evaluate the outcomes of any team activities you led or took part in (for Unit 2 D2 and Unit 4 D2).

You will need these logs and evaluations to help you to complete Task 3 of this assignment.

Task 1 (P6)

Produce a booklet which **describes the different types of teams** found in uniformed public services and the **development stages those teams will go through**.

You may choose to focus on one specific uniformed public service or you may use examples from a range of different services.

Task 2 (P5)

Produce a PowerPoint presentation which **describes evaluation methods used to assess effective team leadership**. (Suggested 10 minutes total delivery time.)

Hand in your slide show after you have presented it with any supporting notes you may have made.

Task 3 (P4, M3, D2)

Use the various logs you have kept throughout the year to show that you have **used appropriate skills when leading a team in the practical implementation of a plan** (P4) **and have demonstrated effective leadership skills to achieve a given task** (M3).

Hand in your log sheets and a statement of the tasks you led and the outcomes with any other supporting evidence (eg observer feedback).

Undertake an **evaluation of your own ability to provide effective team leadership and recommend developments and improvements** (D2).

You can choose how to present your evaluation and development plan based on the pro formas provided for you to log and analyse your performance.

Tutor feedback

Unit 2, Assignment Task 4
By Jackie Jones, BTEC National Year 1

For this task I am going to summarise 3 of the activities where I led a team.

I have actually logged 5 times I was leader and have picked these out as the best examples.

In all 3 activities I have included I helped the team in planning, implementing the plan and achieving the task required. To help me with this I am going to use the logs I made after each of the 3 tasks and an observer feedback sheet produced for one of those tasks. I have also included the video evidence from our team whilst at Clydesdale and a tutor Assessor report for the 100s of boxes task described.

I am then going to evaluate how effective I was as a leader and identify where I need to develop and improve my leadership skills for the future using SWOT and GAP analysis.

As you can see from the log sheets attached, in all the activities the teams I was leading achieved the tasks set. The raft building task required the most planning but in all 3 examples included here the team did plan and largely we followed those plans.

The leadership skills I demonstrated were effective time management, communication and delegation. I also dealt with challenges to my authority as leader and conflict in the team. I supported a hesitant team member (Jennie crossing the lake on the raft). I challenged Jack when he threatened to abandon the task and persuaded him to come back and work with the group.

It would be a good idea to include all five log sheets as when things don't go so well as hoped they provide useful opportunities to learn and develop.

(I know you have used the learning in you personal development planning!)

Self Evaluation Log 1 10 Oct 2006
Jackie Jones, BTEC National Year 1

Details of Team Activity: *The team were given the tasks called 'House of Cards'. Basically it is an activity where we competed with other teams to build a House out of cards and other resources provided in 15 minutes.*
There were 4 people in our team – the teams were selected by using the playing cards and everyone in the same suite went into the same team.

My role in the team (leader)
Our first task was to chose a leader – I think I was chosen because the others know I like doing puzzles. I was very nervous because I'd never led before and the others in the team all seemed more confident.
We had a discussion about possible structures but as the time allowed was so limited in the end we just started building without a clear plan. 2 of the group had done a similar task before so we followed their ideas.

How did I perform?
Overall I think I did quite well, but my role was quite easy because the team worked well together, listened to each other and supported each other and me as leader.

Good honest comment & evaluation.

Yes, not difficult to lead when team want to cooperate!

Tutor feedback

Self Evaluation Log 1 10 Oct 2006
Jackie Jones, BTEC National Year 1 – CONTINUED

How did the team perform? Did we achieve the task?

In the end our House was the winner! We had the tallest house and the structure was both sound and attractive. We were awarded 21/25 points. Our time was not the fastest but we achieved the task within the 15 minutes allowed. We then had to evaluate our team performance and I had to present the flip chart we summarised our ideas on. I was really nervous but because the team had cooperated so well together I really felt OK about doing the presentation.

What were my strengths?

I was good at managing the discussions so that everyone took turns at talking.
I kept a good eye on the time so we achieved the task in the 15 minutes allowed.
I gave a good presentation and answered questions well.

What were my weaknesses?

I lacked confidence and didn't really want to be the leader.
I was nervous before the presentation.

How could I improve my performance?

I need to be more confident.

Student signature: ...J. Jones................ Tutor signature: ...L. Stamore............

Good example of how achieving the best outcome is not just about speed. Shows understanding of task and planning.

But you dealt with both issues!

Self Evaluation Log 2 9 Nov 2006
Jackie Jones, BTEC National Year 1

Details of Team Activity: *This was an outdoor activity. The team were given the task of building a raft from a barrel and some planks and rope and getting everyone safely to the island in the middle of the lake. We had an hour to plan the task and undertake it.*

My role in the team (leader)

I was the leader as we were taking turns during the outdoor activities session and it was my turn.
2 of the boys in the team didn't want me to be leader but the other 2 team members did.

How did I perform?

Eventually it worked out well and I led the team effectively, dealt with the initial conflict over my leadership and the later conflict while we were building the raft and the challenges one team member made to my authority as leader.

How did the team perform? Did we achieve the task?

We did achieve the task in that we built a raft that floated and managed to make the 5 trips to the island that were needed to achieve the task.
We didn't perform brilliantly as a team. There were some squabbles and Jack threatened to go back to the dormitory and not take part.
In the debrief at the end of the task I gave individual feedback to all the team members and made it clear where I thought they had done well (and also not too well!)

What were my strengths?

I surprised myself because usually I don't like dealing with conflict, but I was determined to stay calm and manage the situation.
I explained calmly at the beginning why I felt I was the appropriate leader.
I encouraged effective planning and intervened when an argument started.
I persuaded Jack to stay and join in and supported Jennie who can't swim and didn't want to go on the raft. I insisted everyone had to wear their buoyancy aids even though the boys said they didn't need them.

This was a good example to select as you had to deal with a number of issues including conflict and challenge.

Good honest evaluation here.

Really good evidence of self reflection and personal learning.

Self Evaluation Log 2 9 Nov 2006
Jackie Jones, BTEC National Year 1 – CONTINUED

What were my weaknesses?

The task required understanding how to build a raft and tie knots to keep the structure we built together. Neither of those are my skills but I delegated tasks effective to other team members.

How could I improve my performance?

I could learn to tie knots!

Student signature: ...J. Jones................   Tutor signature: ...L. Stamore.............

Observer feedback Raft Building task 9 Nov 2006
Team leader Jackie, members Jack, Paul, Raj, Jennie

Question	Comments
Were people involved and interested?	Initially not, but Jackie managed the team well and dealt with conflict and with Jack wanting to opt out and Jennie being frightened of the water.
Were members of the group getting satisfaction from being in the group?	Yes, once they settled down and realised that the task could be achieved it they cooperated together.
Was the atmosphere friendly?	There was conflict and bickering which Jackie dealt with. By the end the whole team were proud they had achieved.
What happened when there was conflict? Was it dealt with or ignored?	Jackie dealt with this effectively and quickly so it didn't escalate.
Did some members participate more than others? Who? Why?	Jack didn't contribute much to begin but he came round and joined in well eventually after Jackie spoke to him.
Who carried out the leadership function? How effective were they?	Jackie was the leader. I was impressed with her skills and the quiet but determined way she managed a difficult group.
Who influenced the most?	Paul was the most influential as he had the skills required to build the raft and navigate it.
Were there any rivalries? Did the leader handled them	Not really – the rivalry was with the other teams!
How did the leader organise the planning? Did the team stick to the plan?	Yes, although the detail of the raft building was delegated to Paul as he had the required skills.
Did the leader manage the group and discourage discussion of unrelated matters?	Yes

Jackie, it was a really good idea to include this observation by the instructor at the outdoor activity centre as it completely validates your own log and self evaluation and gives an impartial view of what was happening during this task.

The video evidence also show the group planning and building the raft and crossing to the island.

Tutor feedback

Observer feedback Raft Building task 9 Nov 2006
Team leader Jackie, members Jack, Paul, Raj, Jennie – CONTINUED

Question	Comments
How did the leader manage the decisions making process? How did this affect the group?	*There was a group discussion then the decisions regarding the raft were delegated to Paul. The rota of who would go across to the island when, was decided by Jackie after she had listened to everyone's views.*
Were subgroups formed? How did this affect the task?	*Initially it was a bit boys v girls but Jackie pointed this out and the likely negative impacts this could have.*
How well did the group follow the task instructions?	*Very well except for the reluctance to wear the buoyancy aids.*
Other Comments	*In the end the task was achieved and the team developed into an effective unit supported by Jackie's leadership skills.*

Rob Jackson, Outdoor Activities Instructor, Clydesdale Centre
For reference, a video was taken of all group activities and provided to the college as supporting evidence.

Self Evaluation Log 3 15 Dec 2006
Jackie Jones, BTEC National Year 1

Details of Team Activity:
100s of Boxes. We had to plan a delivery route for a driver delivering boxes to customers and try to ensure the driver's time was used to best effect.

My role in the team (leader)
I was nominated as leader and everyone agreed. They all thought I would be good at managing this task.

How did I perform?
I felt it went well. I encouraged each team member to put forward their ideas and then listen to the others.

How did the team perform? Did we achieve the task?
We achieved the task although our team came 2nd overall.
We listened and worked together.
We cooperated with each other.

What were my strengths?
I encouraged everyone to speak and contribute.
I encouraged listening and cooperation.
I helped the team decide on the approach to take and kept everyone aware of the time.

What were my weaknesses?
I was swayed by Olly who convinced me that his approach was best against my own judgment. If I'd followed my instincts we would have won overall, but as it was a team decision I felt OK about it.

How could I improve my performance?
I should have a stronger belief in myself and my own ideas.

This was a good exercise and my observation record, which you have included, supports your self evaluation in full.

Well done!

ASSESSOR FEEDBACK FORM

Assessor Observation Record	
Learner's name:	Jackie Jones
Programme:	BTEC National Year 1 Public Services
Unit number & title:	UNIT 2 Team Leadership in Uniformed Public Services

Activity observed – Practical Demonstration of Leadership Skills (P4, M3)
The activity was a classroom based task summarised below

Your team are asked to select a leader then:
1. *Plan the trips for a single driver delivering boxes to the towns shown on the Planning Map.*
2. *Complete the driver's time sheet showing the time for driving, unloading and on break and also the total time at work.*
3. *Enter each stage of the operation separately on the time sheet.*
4. *Once the task is completed debrief and evaluate your team performance.*

How the activity meets the requirements of the unit grading criteria

P4 use appropriate skills to lead a team in the practical implementation of a plan
M3 demonstrate effective leadership skills when leading a team in the practical implementation of a plan to achieve a given task.

Jackie was chosen unanimously as leader – Sam summarised the reason as 'you're good at these puzzle type tasks'.
Jackie encouraged the team to read the instructions carefully and review the planning map and time sheet.
She encouraged each of the four team members to give their views and ideas. She intervened when Sam and Paul were both talking at the same time.
Jackie worked with the team at trying out some possible approaches. She kept her eye on the time and made the team aware of deadlines.
The task was achieved in the 2nd fastest time.
Jackie debriefed the team effectively and led the group in an evaluation of their performance.

Candidate	Jackie Jones
Assessor	Laura Stanmore
Date	15 Dec 2006

Personal Leadership SWOT analysis by Jackie Jones	
Strengths	**Weaknesses**
• *Good listener* • *Good time keeper in team activities* • *Sometimes prepared to challenge poor motivation* • *Able to support anxious team members* • *Well organised* • *Can delegate effectively* • *When I completed the McGregor X/Y questionnaire I scored 38 which shows I believe in motivating and encouraging the team*	• *Lack confidence* • *Don't like giving oral presentations* • *Get irritated with team members who mess around* • *Not as physically fit as I need to be for outdoor team events* • *Avoided managing conflict in one leadership situation* • *Maybe too trusting and don't have sufficient authority as leader*
Opportunities	**Threats**
• *My BTEC programme has given me lots of opportunities to develop and apply new skills* • *The outdoor activities week next term will provide more chance to act as leader*	• *My lack of confidence might let me down* • *I have got behind with my assignment work and need to manage my own time better*
How can your weakness be addressed and threats turned into opportunities? 1. I need to be more patient with others and think about ways to motivate reluctant team members 2. I need to follow my fitness programme better to ensure I can make a full contribution as both a team member and team leader 3. I have got 2 presentations to do at college next week and will practise hard to improve how I do and also be more confident in delivering the presentation as this skill can transfer to my ability to brief and debrief a team with authority 4. I have learned from the task I didn't lead very effectively that I must always challenge poor performance and conflict in the team 5. My score in the McGregor X/Y approach may suggest I'm too trusting.	

Jackie, you have undertaken an honest self evaluation here and shown that you are aware of the aspects of effective leadership that you need to develop and build on.

Jackie Jones – GAP Analysis

Step One: Define where you want to be – your goal

Describe what it will feel like when you have achieved your goal
1. My first goal is to be a confident and effective leader when we go on the outdoor activities week and in all future tasks
2. My long term goal is uni and a career in the Police Service

Step Two: Clarify where you are

Where are you now? What are your key strengths and identified development needs?
I have identified my strengths and development needs in the SWOT analysis I have completed

Step Three: Identify enablers and constraints

Enablers (things that will help me achieve my goals) are:
My wish to do really well on BTEC National and maybe get to University
My determination to apply to the Police Service and be able to show how I meet their leadership and team competence requirements

Constraints (things that will get in the way of achieving my goals) are:
Low confidence and being perceived as lacking authority when leading
Reluctance to challenge unmotivated or disruptive team members

Step Four: Prioritise

To strengthen your enablers and diminish the impact of the constraints you need to prioritise – what should you work on first?
1. Building confidence and self belief in my leadership ability
2. Challenging early and actively motivating teams I lead

Step Five: Plan action

Key Issue 1 Confidence and personal authority	*Required Action* Volunteer to take the lead whenever the opportunity arises both in college and in other settings	*Who Is Involved* Me and any team members when I'm acting as leader	*Review Date* After Residential week in April
Key Issue 2 Challenging and motivating	*Required Action* Identify where issues are building in the team and take the initiative eg by holding team briefings to motivate team members	*Who Is Involved* Me and any team members when I'm acting as leader	*Review Date* After Residential week in April

Jackie, you have drawn up a clear plan of action which should build on the strengths you have already demonstrated as an effective team leader.

You will get lots more opportunities to take the leadership role during the rest of your BTEC National programme!

ASSESSOR FEEDBACK FORM

BTEC National Uniformed Public Service
UNIT 2 Team Leadership in Uniformed Public Services
Assignment Practical Demonstration of Leadership Skills
Jackie Jones, BTEC National Year 1

Task 4 (P4, M3, D2)

Tutor feedback

Task 4

Jackie, you have included a good range of evidence of your role as team leader and how the teams you have led have planned and achieved the tasks set for them.

Your own self evaluations are supported by an Observer feedback from the instructor at Clydesdale and the video of the team, plus my Assessor observation record of the 100s of Boxes activity.

You could have included an evaluation by team members too? Also some of the photos taken in class?

Your SWOT and GAP analyses show that you understand the skills and qualities needed to be an effective team leader and are aware of your achievements and development needs in this role.

A well thought out assignment. Make sure you follow through on the review identified on the GAP analysis (put it in your diary)!

Grading criteria achieved
P4, M3, D2

UNIT 5 – Understanding Discipline within the Uniformed Public Services

SAMPLE ASSIGNMENT

Types of authority and the importance of authority in the uniformed public services.

BACKGROUND INFORMATION

Working in the uniformed public services is a career many people aspire to. However, it is not the ideal career for everyone because members of the uniformed public services have to be able to accept discipline and orders and acknowledge the rank structures and authority systems in the service they join. This does not mean that they blindly obey orders where they see a conflict of values or interests, but that they understand the due processes that have to be followed in all dealings with their commanding officers and the general public.

This assignment will enable you to show that you can:

> *P5 describe four types of authority*
>
> *P6 explain the nature of authority in relation to the uniformed public services*
>
> *M4 explain the importance of recognising authority and the consequences of a lack of authority within the uniformed public services.*

Remember that you must list your reference sources at the end of your work in a bibliography. This list should include the titles of websites and newspapers or magazines you have used, the titles and authors of textbooks you have referred to, and information on any other public services booklets or documents you have quoted from or used for reference.

Task 1

Produce an information sheet or leaflet **explaining the nature of authority** in relation to the uniformed public services (P6) and **describing at least four types of authority** (P5).

Your leaflet will be given out to other potential students at a careers fair to be held next term.

Task 2

Write an article for the college student newspaper which **explains the importance of recognising authority and the consequences of a lack of authority** within the uniformed public services (M4).

PASS LEVEL ANSWER

Types of Authority and how they are used in uniformed public services, by Shamir Amed BTEC National Year 1

The principle of authority is that in every organised group the supreme authority must lie somewhere. Lines of authority must be clear to everyone including who has the ultimate authority.

Authority is based on the understanding and acceptance of the rights and abilities of legitimate bodies to set boundaries and enforce norms of behaviour and rules.

Good definitions – where did you find these? You have not referenced them.

Authoritarian

This is a type of authority where the individual that task would effect doesn't get consulted and doesn't have any input into any of the ideas to the solution.

Authoritarian usually uses rewards as a incentive to completing the tasks and punishments or sanctions if the task is not successfully completed.

The uniformed public services use this type of authority because it gets things done without messing about for example in an emergency like if there was a riot at a prison the Control and Restraint team would go in and the person in charge would expect the rest of the team to obey orders without question.

Appropriate example but avoid slang (messing about).

Rational Authority

Rational Authority is due to the abilities and the experience of the individual whom it concerns.

The only way to gain Rational Authority is gaining expert Knowledge and expert abilities throughout a career. It's related to having respect for someone because they have done the job and have the experience and so if they ask someone they manage to do a specific job, or to do things in a specific way the team member will trust their judgement because they have experience and knowledge.

Public services example?

Legal Authority

Legal authority is specifically established by the law for the purposes of social regulation and control

In democratic societies we say we have 'the rule of law'.

A good example of this is a police officer who has authority in public because of their job. The law defines the police powers (in PACE) and so long as the police act within the law as laid down by parliament they have the right to exercise legal authority.

Good example.

Should refer to PACE 1984 & other relevant legislation and regulations.

Dictatorial Authority

This is exercised by a dictator and is imposed on people without them having any say in what happens.

Stalin was a Russian dictator who imposed his will by fear and intimidation. This is a negative type of authority.

Consultative Authority

This is where the leader consults with the team and asks their views for example on solving a problem, but in the end the leader will make the decision.

This may be because the leader has a better understanding of the bigger picture or because they don't really want to listen so do what they had planned anyway.

Democratic Authority

In this approach the leader lets everyone make a contribution and come to a team solution to the problem. This can only work where there is time for everyone to discuss things and come to agreement on their plan of action.

Authority and the uniformed public services

Authority is the ability to make somebody do something that is sometimes against their interests.

In the uniformed public services a superior officer has the authority to order someone less powerful than themselves to complete a task that they don't want to do themselves. Authority is usually given to someone because of their experience.

Authority is strongly hierarchal, as it always goes down the hierarchy triangle and never goes up it – authority comes from the top.

Authority is relevant to the uniformed public services because it gives them more power over the general public so they can do their jobs properly. For example a police officer would have Authority in the general public because of their job and would be the first one asked, if there was a problem. They also have the authority to request the public to do things or if necessary make them so for example if there was a car crash they could order onlookers to leave the scene and if there was a fight or a raid in a club they could order the people there to stay and if necessary arrest them so they obeyed the orders.

Would this ever have relevance to uniformed public services? Would it ever be appropriate to use in such services?

Rather a negative view!

Public services example?

Use in uniformed public services?

Not necessarily!

Leaders can delegate appropriately – they can ask team members to do tasks that free up their own time to do management tasks.

You really need to develop this with some specific examples.

ASSESSOR FEEDBACK FORM

BTEC National Uniformed Public Service
UNIT 5 Understanding Discipline in the Uniformed Public Services
Shamir Amed, BTEC National Diploma Year 1

Task 1 (P5, P6)

Tutor feedback

Shamir, you have described different types of authority and have used some uniformed public service examples to support your comments.

You need to develop your examples further to fully meet the P6 criteria. See comments on your assignment.

You have not handed Task 2 in – is there a reason for this? We did cover this topic in class so you should have had some notes to start your research for this grading criteria.

You have not included any references – you have clearly quoted from sources you found – what were these?

Grading criteria achieved
P5 only achieved
P6 is referred
M4 was not submitted
Please resubmit when you have reviewed and completed your work – within one month of this feedback.

MERIT LEVEL ANSWER

Unit 5, Assignment Task 1 Identifying Authority, by By Simon Eyres

In this leaflet I am going to explain what authority means in the uniformed public services and describe a range of different types of authority.

Nice introductory statement.

What is authority?

Authority is having the ability and the right to control and order people. If you have authority you have an amount of power but it is not power. You can have power without authority.

Not just people but situations too?

Traditionally a distinction has been made between INTRINSIC authority which is also known as personal power and may be unpredictable since it is personal and forceful.

This is true – but I'm not sure by the way you have worded it if you really understand this or have copied it – you should reference quotations.

EXTRINSIC authority operates with external guarantees, there is delegated power exercised by an individual who may wear a uniform or have some other outward sign of their authority to be undertaking a task or role. This delegated power comes from the framework of society as a whole so the person exercising extrinsic authority is a spokesperson or representative of society and the structure society has decided on.

There are different types of authority these are:

- Dictatorial
- Authoritarian
- Democratic or Participative
- Legal
- Consultative

This would be better placed after the next section.

How is authority used in the uniformed public services?

Authority is used in all uniformed public services and any other job. It is a way of upholding discipline. It is used in the uniformed public services to keep it running in a professional way, an example of when it is used is in the hierarchy of authority (chain of command). The higher up the chain you are, the more authority you possess. But even the top person in each uniformed public service is accountable to the government and the public at large through parliament and the various Inspectorates that oversee their service.

Good explanation of accountability for those who can exercise authority in public services.

It is also important in the uniformed public services because everyone (including the general public) needs to know where the orders come down from and who to see if they need someone of higher authority. For example, in the police it is important to know you have authority over the general public and for the general public to acknowledge that.

Good point – authority would break down if society did not accept it.

Democratic participative authority

This is where the person of higher authority describes the situation to everyone involved and encourages input for the solution. This means that the democratic leader will say what they are planning to do and ask for input from people below.

They will ask for input and opinions to see how they feel it should be dealt with. Then the higher authority will choose what is the best way to solve the situation using the input given to them as commander.

It is sometimes used in the police if they are planning a raid. A higher authority will tell the police officers what is being planed and will ask for their opinions on how it should be handled and then find a solution using the input from the fellow officers.

This type of authority uses reward and shared goals to achieve the desired solution.

Our election process give chance to participate and those who are elected have the authority we give to them.

Dictatorial Authority

This is where the authority is carried out without the consent of the individuals of who it effects. This means the person may or may not agree to it what they are being told is going to happen, it will still be carried out regardless.

This form of authority should never be used in the uniformed public services. It is a misuse of power as it is applied using threats and punishments, an example of this is Hitler in world war two, where he decided to exterminate all the Jews. His followers accepted this view as right and carried out his orders.

This authority is often seen it is a form of intimidation as the higher authority uses it to intimidate the people below into conforming with what they want to do so with Hitler, his followers knew that if they didn't carry out his orders it might be them and their families sent to the death camps.

This type of authority is used by all types of extreme state administrations and can be seen right throughout history.

It requires blind obedience from those it rules or they are punished. They are not allowed to question if things are right or wrong – they must just do as they have been told regardless.

Authoritarian authority

This is where individuals are told what to do and how to do it without input or consulting. It is where you are told to go and do something and you go away and do it without asking questions or inputting you own opinions. This form is frequently used in the uniformed public services, especially the training processes.

154

Good example although it could be worded better!

Good link to concept of authority in a democracy.

Good contrast with what you have just described.

Good! Clear rationale why this would be inappropriate in a public service

Yes!

This is used in the army during the training process to train the recruits so the fitness instructor will tell the recruits to go on a run or do something else and they are not allowed to question or ask why?

Not sure of the relevance of this example?

This is a form of authoritarian authority. This form of authority uses rewards to gain what is needed from the person or persons. It is a way of getting what needs to be done, done quickly and effectively.

It is also used in emergency situations by the uniformed public services so the person in charge gives out the orders and the people they command obey them. For example the police controlling a riot at a protest or football match; prison officers dealing with disruptive prisoners; the armed forces in face to face combat.

Good examples.

Legal authority

This is established by law for the purpose of social regulations and control. This means people that have authority over the public to keep order and control within society. This is the main authority used by the uniformed public services.

The police have legal authority as they are key in upholding legal authority, as they are the main service that upholds the law and protects the public, If a police officer stops a member of the public for being anti-social this is legal authority being used. But police have to operate within the rules such as PACE 1984 and Police Act 1997. They also have to obey the Police Code of Conduct.

Excellent!

This form of authority uses punishment for law being broken but the punishments in a democratic state have been decided by the law making process of their parliament, not by the uniformed public services themselves – the members of the uniformed public services are carrying out the wishes of the democratic government of the UK.

Really good understanding shown here.

Consultative authority

This is where the leader shares the situation with their team but not the solution.

The leader consults with the team to reach an agreed outcome. Sometimes in the uniformed public services this is a good approach especially if there is time to consult and the outcomes are not critical, but often decisions have to be taken urgently and the outcomes could be fatal if the wrong decision was taken.

Valid points made.

In those situations wasting time on consulting could lead to loss of morale as leaders look weak.

Task 2 The importance of recognising authority and the consequences of a lack of authority.

In this article I am going to explain the importance of authority in the uniformed public services by using some real examples mainly based around the Armed Forces and their authority to engage in actions in the UK and abroad and what happens when military action is not properly authorised and the conduct of police officers.

Firstly for the armed forces to engage in any action it has to be authorised by their military commanders acting in agreement with the government (the Defence Secretary, the Prime minister and the Cabinet). If it is on an international scene it also has to be authorised through the United Nations. The UK's action in Afghanistan was justified as quoted here.

We are there under the authority of a UN resolution, at the request of a democratic elected government, and with the support of the local people. Speech by Des Browne MP, Secretary of State for Defence, at the Royal United Services Institute, 19th September 2006.

Sometimes the authority taken by the military can be misused – recently US Military personnel were accused of abusing inmates at Iraq's Abu Ghraib prison in 2003 and 2004. They faced a number of charges including dereliction of duty, conspiracy and assault.

Their defence argued that they were obeying senior officers and their orders. There was, claimed the defence, an ambiguous chain of command with multiple military intelligence components and civilian intelligence components with conflicting rules. Despite these claims 11 US personnel have been found guilty of abuse of prisoners.

General Mark Kimmitt said 'We're appalled. These are our fellow soldiers. and they represent us. They wear the same uniform as us, and they let their fellow soldiers down... and if we can't hold ourselves up as an example of how to treat people with dignity and respect ... We can't ask that other nations do that to our soldiers as well...So what would I tell the people of Iraq? This is wrong. This is reprehensible. But this is not representative of the 150,000 soldiers that are over here. I'd say the same thing to the American people... Don't judge your army based on the actions of a few.'

All uniformed public services have complaints processes and have bodies to investigate complaints and make recommendations. The UK Armed forces are subject to UK criminal law – this means that when they are serving in UK they have the same status as any other UK citizen in terms of how they are treated if they commit an offence under civilian law.

Also the armed forces are often sent to work overseas. In many cases, such deployments are to areas which are unstable, often hostile and sometimes where law and order is applied very differently to the UK system. To deal with this The Armed Forces Act received Royal Assent on 8 Nov 06. The primary

Good choice of services to illustrate your article.

Clear authority lines for the armed forces shown.

Good example of the legitimacy of action being claimed.

Good example – could you have used a UK example instead?

A good quotation to use to explain the importance of authority being properly exercised.

Source?

Good summary.

purpose of this Act is to harmonise and streamline the discipline systems of the Royal Navy, Army and Royal Air Force and ensure that UK Armed Forces have a modern military justice system. Having one set of clear laws and procedures removes any doubt as to which system service personnel are subject to.

The main points are:-

- A single system of Service Law
- A unified court martial system, including a joint service prosecuting authority
- A new grievance procedure for members of the armed forces
- A new system of statutory inquiries

The police and their code of conduct. *This states that an officer cannot break the law and then use as a defence the fact that he or she did so in order to carry out their duties. Where there is evidence that an officer has committed a criminal offence, whether in the course of their duty or otherwise, they can be charged and taken before a court. If found guilty, they would be punished in just the same way as anyone convicted of a criminal offence. The Code of Conduct sets the standards of behaviour which officers are expected to follow when carrying out their duties and, to a lesser extent, in their private lives. The Code covers a range of misdemeanours from fairly trivial things to serious matters such as neglect of duty and oppressive conduct.*

Where a complaint is received from a member of the public about the behaviour of an officer or a police staff member, or facts come to light, which suggest that an officer may have committed a criminal offence or a breach of the Code of Conduct, the matter will be investigated. A senior officer can deal with less serious cases locally provided that, in the case of complaints, the person making the complaint agrees.

The police code of conduct states (amongst other things) that *Use of force and abuse of authority:- Officers must never knowingly use more force than is reasonable, nor should they abuse their authority.*

Although society has delegated authority to personnel in the uniformed services (which is exercised via the chain of command in those services) that authority has to be used responsibly, it cannot be used to justify abuse or bad behaviour by the specific member of the uniformed service or by their superior officers. All personnel in the uniformed public services have an obligation to use authority well and uphold the law.

If they see others doing wrong they should report them. This is hard as it is seen as letting down your friends and colleagues. It is known as 'whistle blowing'. If a member of the public services sees corruption and does not report it they are seen as also guilty because by not reporting they appear to be complicit with wrong doing and abuse of power. Most uniformed public services have whistle blowing policies which allow personnel to report suspected breaches of codes of conduct without being publicly identified. Under The Public Interest Disclosure Act 1999 employees are obliged to disclose to their employers situations where, amongst other things there are:-

- actual or potential damage to the public interest
- to avert actual or potential disaster

Well done – good to see up-to-date legislation being referred to.

Good.

Presume this is a quote?

Reference?

Good.

This is an interesting approach to have taken.

I know we did not cover this in class so well done for introducing it to your assignment.

- financial malpractice
- miscarriage of justice
- misconduct is being covered up or you believe that there will be attempts to cover-up

A recent allegation of police corruption saw a Detective in Nottinghamshire jailed for passing on information to known criminals in return for designer clothes. A Police Federation's chairman said the corruption case had major implications. The jailed detective gave information to certain figures within the criminal fraternity as to what police action was being taken against them and what police tactics were being used to bring them to justice so putting his colleagues in extreme danger because those criminals will stop short of no level of violence to prevent themselves being arrested or locked up. He was running the risk of those officers being murdered. Police forces are run on trust and when trust goes everything falls apart.

http://en.wikipedia.org/wiki/Abu_Ghraib_prisoner_abuse
http://news.bbc.co.uk/   http://www.mod.uk/   http://www.ipcc.gov.uk/

Consequence of misuse of authority.

How was this uncovered?

Was it whistle - blowing?

Other references used?

Please ensure you include everything!

ASSESSOR FEEDBACK FORM

BTEC National Uniformed Public Service
UNIT 5 Understanding Discipline in the Uniformed Public Services
Simon Eyres, BTEC National Diploma Year 1

Task 1 (P5, P6), Task 2 (M4)

Tutor feedback

Simon, this assignment shows clear evidence of research and the use of your research applied to specific examples from the uniformed public services.

Task 1

You have described types of authority and have explained how these apply in uniformed public services.

Task 2

You have explained the importance of recognising authority in uniformed public services with some clear examples from the armed forces and police. You have also found some real, relevant and up-to-date examples of breaches of authority and explained the impact of these.

You have identified legislation by which society both delegates authority to specific uniformed public services and encourages reporting of breaches of authority. You have also explained how uniformed public services are held accountable for their exercise of authority. Please read the feedback on your assignment carefully as there are some points where improvements could be made – please bear these in mind when writing future assignments, especially referencing your sources in full.

Grading criteria achieved P5, P6, M4 – well done!

UNIT 7 – Physical Preparation and Fitness for the Uniformed Services

SAMPLE ASSIGNMENT

Planning a personal fitness training programme.

BACKGROUND INFORMATION

Workers in the uniformed public services need to be physically fit, as their roles are usually very active and physically demanding. There are fitness entry requirements which are tested and many uniformed public services also test personnel annually to ensure their fitness is maintained.

In this assignment you will be devising a training programme to prepare yourself for a selected uniformed public service.

This assignment will enable you to show that you can:

> *P4 plan a personal fitness training programme to prepare for a selected uniformed public service, with support*
>
> *M3 plan a personal fitness training programme to prepare for uniformed public service.*

Remember that you must list your reference sources at the end of your work in a bibliography. This list should include the titles of websites and newspapers or magazines you have used, the titles and authors of textbooks you have referred to, and information on any other uniformed public services booklets or documents you have quoted from or used for reference.

Task 1 (P4, M3)

Having undertaken the police entry fitness test you will be aware of the requirements and your current level of fitness.

Setting your goal as achieving the required fitness level for your chosen uniformed public service and bearing in mind both current fitness and specific requirements for your chosen service, **plan a personal fitness training programme** to prepare you for applying for your chosen service.

It is suggested that your training plan includes some explanation of why you have chosen particular activities and how these will help you to improve your own personal fitness level.

It is suggested that you produce a plan for four weeks (after which you should aim to retake the police test and see if your fitness has improved).

159

REFER LEVEL ANSWER

Josie Evans, BTEC National Yr 1

Fitness Training Plan

I have produced a full training programme to improve results or to get myself to the required standard of the entry requirements for a Uniformed Public Service fitness text.

I have undertook the endurance test and reached level 5.4, this is the exact level you need to past the test however I am going to develop a training programme which will help me improve on my fitness level.

My training programme

WEEK ONE

Monday: Circuit Training for I hr: 5mins jogging, 5mins warm ups - dynamic stretching such as hand down spine, shoulder strangle, quadriceps standing and normal stretch. 45 minutes playing a main sport e.g. badminton. 5 minutes cool down stretches

Tuesday: Weight: Strength building for 45 mins

Wednesday: Swimming 25 lengths of the pool and I hr playing main sport of choice.

Thursday: Weight training for strength for 45 mins

Friday: 10 minutes warm up techniques, half mile run and 10 minutes cool down techniques.

Saturday: Circuit Training for I hr: 5mins jogging, 5mins warm ups – dynamic stretching such as hand down spine, shoulder strangle, quadriceps standing and normal stretch. 45 minutes playing a main sport e.g. badminton. 5 minutes cool down stretches. Plus 20 sit ups and 20 push ups

Sunday: Rest or Flexibility for 30mins

WEEK 2

Monday: Circuit Training for 1.5 hr: 5mins jogging, 5mins warm ups – dynamic stretching such as hand down spine, shoulder strangle, quadriceps standing and normal stretch. I hr and 15 minutes playing two main sports e.g. badminton. And football. 5 minutes cool down stretches

Tuesday: weight training e.g. weight machines.

Wednesday: Swimming 40 lengths of a swimming pool in the morning and 30 minutes of trampolining in the evening.

Thursday: weight training for strength e.g. weight machine

Jo, which test did you take?

What does that test involve?

Which service are you hoping to join?

Does it have the same fitness requirements?

You have included a range of different types of training – what aspects of fitness are you hoping to develop through each of these activities?

Weight training – for how long?

What specific training will you do?

What are you hoping to achieve by this?

Friday: 1 mile run with warm up dynamic stretching before and cool downs after exercise.

Saturday: Rest or flexibility for one hour

Sunday: Rest

WEEK 3

Monday: Circuit training for 2hrs. With warm up techniques at the beginning then playing two main sports for an hour each with a rest in between. And cool down techniques after exercises.

Tuesday: Weight training in the morning and half a mile run in the evening.

Wednesday: Swimming 45 lengths and an hour of trampolining in the evening.

Thursday: weight training and a half a mile run in the evening.

Friday: 1 mile run with warm up dynamic stretching before and cool downs after exercise.

Saturday: play basketball for 2 hrs and flexibility for half a hour.

Sunday: Rest or flexibility for an hour.

WEEK 4

Monday: Circuit training for 2 hrs. With warm up techniques at the beginning then playing two main sports for an hour each with a rest in between. And cool down techniques after exercises.

Tuesday: Weight training in the morning and a mile run. And in the evening 30 sit ups and 30 push-ups

Wednesday: Swimming 50 lengths a hour trampolining with 35 push ups and 35 sit ups

Thursday: a mile and a half run with weight training.

Friday: Circuit training for 2hrs. With warm up techniques at the beginning then playing two main sports for an hour each with a rest in between. And cool down techniques after exercises. With 25 sit ups and 25 push ups.

Saturday: Circuit training for 2hrs with warm ups and cool downs. Exercises such as step ups, push ups and sit ups. With a mile run in the evening.

Sunday: 35 sit-ups and 35 push-ups with a hour flexibility in the evening.

Tutor feedback

Do you plan to rest on both Sat and Sun?

Why?

How will you decide whether to rest or do flexibility training?

What are you hoping to achieve in your flexibility training?

Why?

What actions will you take after completing your training?

ASSESSOR FEEDBACK FORM

BTEC National Uniformed Public Service
UNIT 7 Physical Preparation and Fitness for the Uniformed Services
Josie Evans, BTEC National Year 1

Task 1 (P4, M3)

Tutor feedback

Task 1

Jo, you have given some thought to this task and have produced a training plan that should develop a range of skills and improve your personal fitness.

I would like you to review the comments I have written on your work as it is not clear WHY you have chosen specific training activities or how these will help you improve your personal fitness.

Which uniformed public service you are aspiring to join?

What implications do the fitness tests for that service have on your training schedule?

Grading criteria achieved
Refer
Please resubmit within four weeks after amending as per feedback on your assignment.

MERIT LEVEL ANSWER

My Training Programme for Uniformed Public Services by Krys Ciros BTEC National Year 1

What service do I want to join? What is my GOAL!

My chosen service that I want to join is the prison service.

Aim of the programme

I have taken the entry tests for fitness for the Police whilst at college. While this is different to the Prison Service tests it does indicate my current fitness level.

Good justification for undertaking personal fitness training.

The aim of this training programme is to see if I can improve my result in the bleep test to a level 6. The level I am at now is 5.4, this is a pass in the police force, but I would like to have a higher level, due to 5.4 being the minimum level of fitness to join the police. Having a slightly higher level will increase my chance of being accepted into any uniformed service and be less stressful for me.

The pre entry Fitness Tests For HM Prison Service

Grip strength test

This is where the participants are required to squeeze a measuring device as tight as you can – this test must be passed.

Good summary of tests and what is being tested.

163

Endurance test

This requires the participant to run faster and faster over a 15m track until you reach the pass requirement. This tests your stamina (aerobic) fitness and aerobic endurance is essential to good health – this is why this test has to be taken and passed.

Dyno test

This requires the participant to complete a set number of pulls and pushes on a dyno machine. This test measures the strength of your upper body and lower body. This test must also be passed.

Speed agility test

This requires the participant to run with obstacles in their way and having to change direction. This test is done because prison officers have to be able to respond as quickly as possible when incidents occur therefore this test must be passed.

Shield test

This requires the participant to hold a 6kg shield during control and restraint techniques. This test must also be passed.

Types of training to be used:

When planning this training programme I took account of the need to develop flexibility, aerobic fitness, stamina, and long distance running. All of these will be useful in the prison service. I considered various training techniques, which need to be considered when designing a fitness training programme and working towards my goals. This 4 week training programme should be evaluated to see what impact it has had before being repeated. After completing it I will retake the police tests through college.

In all fitness training you should remember the FITT criteria. I have used this is devising my own programme.

Good rationale here.

Always worth keeping in mind!

	Term	Meaning	Standard recommendation
F	Frequency	How often you exercise	5–6 times per week
I	Intensity	How hard you exercise	Moderate to high
T	Time	How long you exercise	Anywhere from 15 to 40 minutes
T	Type	The kind of exercise you undertake	Most exercise, from brisk walking to high intensity sports

STRENGTH TRAINING

The main purpose of strength training is to build strength in your muscles and the best way to accomplish this is to follow a programme using weights or weight machines. This is also known as resistance training as it uses resistance e.g. weights to train against. There are various muscle contraction exercises to think about such as Isometric, this is muscle activity held at a fixed length, an example of this would be holding an object at arms length.

SPEED TRAINING

Speed is the ability to move a part of the body quickly and when practised at speed the neurons then improve their speed at moving the muscles. Speed depends on the following factors mobility/flexibility, strength, muscle endurance and skill. To train for speed you therefore have to train for strength, stamina and suppleness.

Good summary of the different types of training you may have considered when putting your personal programme together.

STAMINA TRAINING

There are two types of Stamina Training and these are cardio-vascular endurance, which involves the ability to swim, walk, run etc for long periods of time. This work is done by the heart and can be kept up for an extended period of time. The other Stamina Training is muscle endurance and this is the ability of a muscle to repeat an action several times.

SUPPLENESS TRAINING

Suppleness training is an important part of your fitness regime if you want to improve your stretching techniques and flexibility.

SKILL TRAINING

Most activities involve some kind of skill, which can be learnt by practising the activity. Fitness training also aids to develop your skill as strength, suppleness, speed and stamina allow you to perform more efficiently.

AGILITY TRAINING

Agility simply means to move quickly and nimble and is a combination of speed, balance, co-ordination and strength. As a result, speed and strength training are important when developing agility and flexibility training can develop co-ordination and balance.

CARDIO-VASCULAR TRAINING

Cardiovascular training uses the muscles of the heart and involves aerobic, stamina and endurance fitness. CV includes the ability to run, walk, swim etc for long periods of time, this is important in the uniformed services as it is one of the main factors of all round fitness. The energy for CV work comes from oxygen, which is why it is also called aerobic fitness (with oxygen). Running is seen as the most effective type of CV work.

My Fitness Plan – Week 1

Monday – 3 minute slow jogging to raise the heart rate and get oxygen to the muscles. Stretches (as indicated) Moderate paced jog for 9 minutes – improving aerobic fitness. 30 seconds sprint – to improve aerobic fitness and to raise heart rate. 3 minute cool down jog – lowers the heart rate, relaxes the muscles to prevent lactic acid (aching in the muscles). Basic stretch to allow the muscles to relax. Reps 1

Tuesday – Rest

Weds – 3 minutes slow jogging to raise the heart rate and get oxygen to the muscles. Stretches (as indicated) Moderate paced jog for 10 minutes – improving aerobic fitness and to raise heart rate. 3 minute cool down jog – lowers the heart rate, relaxes the muscles to prevent lactic acid (aching in the muscles). Basic stretch to allow the muscles to relax. Reps 1

Thursday – Rest

Friday – 5 minutes slow jogging to raise the heart rate and the temperature, also to get oxygen to the muscles. Stretch. Bleep test – work to a level that

165

Good explanation as to why you have included each activity and what you hope to achieve in each one.

You have not explained why you have planned three rest days in week 1 but only two in subsequent weeks.

is comfortable, push to aim for level 3. 2 minutes brisk walking to relax the muscles and calm the breathing down, slower therefore not panting. Stretch. Reps 1

Saturday – Swim one length of the pool, to warm up the muscles and heart rate. Stretches. Swim 30 lengths of the pool at a constant pace continuously – improving aerobic fitness for 1.5 mile run. Stretching.

Sunday – Rest

Week 2

Monday – 5 minutes slow Jogging to raise the heart rate and the temperature, also to get oxygen to the muscles. Stretch. Bleep test – work to a level that is comfortable, push to aim for level 3. 2 minutes brisk walking to relax the muscles and calm the breathing down, slower therefore not panting. Stretch. Reps 1

Tuesday – Rest

Wednesday – 8 minutes slow jogging to raise the heart rate and to get oxygen to the muscles. Improving aerobic fitness and stamina. Stretches. Reps 2

Thursday – 20 minute jog to improve aerobic fitness. 2 minute walk to relax and lower the heart rate. Stretch. Reps 1

Friday – 7 minute slow jogging to raise the heart rate and the temperature of the body. Get oxygen to the muscles while working. Stretch. Bleep test – work to a level that is comfortable, aim to beat the 3.5 level or 4.0. 2 minutes brisk walking to relax the muscles and cool down the breathing. Walk for 1 minute – stretches. Reps 1

Saturday – Ice Dancing – 1 hour and 30 minutes – working the legs and using, power, strength, agility. To move around on the ice at speed and maintain balance. Stretches.

Sunday – Rest

Week 3

Monday – Walk up 60 stairs. Stretch. Jog for 18 minutes. Walk briskly for 3 minutes to lower heart rate. Stretch. Reps 3

Tuesday – Netball – Jog for 2 minutes to warm the muscles and raise the heart rate. Stretches. 45 minutes in a game of netball with other candidates. 1 minute walk to reduce heart rate to a suitable resting level.

Wednesday – Ice dancing – 2 hours – practicing different moves and shapes while on ice, practice routines and use arms and legs to co ordinate with each other. Stretches. Improve in speed and agility to stay balanced on the ice and present a reasonably stable figure

Good awareness of safe training principles here.

Intensity of training is gradually building up – good!

Thursday – Rest

Friday – Warm up for 7 minutes. Stretches. Play a game of badminton for 45 minutes in a pair or group. Stretches. Walk for 2 minutes to reduce heart rate to a suitable resting level.

Saturday – Walk for 2 minutes, 10 squats to get the blood moving through the legs, then practice shapes and transitions on horse back. Improve shapes and transitions. Work on routines to present with no corrections needed. Reps 3

Sunday – Rest

Week 4

Monday – Warm up for 10 minutes. Stretches. Dance to music. Learn half of a routine for a dance and improve on the skills all ready learnt. Make the dance presentable as more than one person or as a group of people. Cool down for 10 mins to reduce heart rate and temperature and to reduce the chance of lactic acid. Stretches. Reps 2

Tuesday – Ice dancing – 2 hours – practicing different moves and shapes while on ice, practice routines and use arms and legs to co ordinate with each other. Stretches. Improve in speed and agility to stay balanced on the ice and present a reasonably stable figure.

Wednesday – Rest

Thursday – Walk for 2 minutes, 13 squats to get the blood moving through the legs, and then work on lunging with the horse on a long rein and in a 25 meter circle practicing voice commands and transitions. Reps 2

Friday – Swim one length of the pool, to warm up the muscles and heart rate. Stretches. Swim 40 lengths of the pool continuously – improving aerobic fitness for 1.5 mile run. Swim one length in every 3 at faster speed – this will improve stamina, aerobic and anaerobic fitness. Stretching.

Saturday – Netball – Jog for 3 minutes to warm the muscles and raise the heart rate. Stretches. 55 minutes in a game of netball with other students. 2 minute walk to reduce heart rate to a suitable resting level

Sunday – Rest

Now I must review my fitness and see what improvements I have made.

I may need to review or change my programme (depending on what tests for the prison service I now need to work on) but will certainly need to keep a training programme going – it's hard to build up fitness and once done, regular training is needed to maintain this level of fitness.

167

Good final summary statement here.

ASSESSOR FEEDBACK FORM

BTEC National Uniformed Public Service
UNIT 7 Physical Preparation and Fitness for the Uniformed Services
Krys Ciros, BTEC National Year 1

Task 1 (P4, M3)

Tutor feedback

Task 1

Well done, Krys, this is very good work. You have clearly identified your goal in this training programme.

You have identified what you will need to do to improve your fitness for the police test and why you want to do this even though you would just meet the entry requirement.

You have explained the types of fitness training you might select.

Your four week programme gives a good range of activities and a justification for your choice of each.

Please do read the comments on your work – you deserve to be pleased with your assignment!

Grading criteria achieved
P4
M3